WALKING IN LIGHT
TRUE LIFE IN 1 JOHN

Brooke Holt

Bible Study Media

Published in Houston, Texas by Bible Study Media, Inc.

WALKING IN LIGHT

TRUE LIFE IN 1 JOHN

© 2021 Brooke Holt. All rights reserved.

Published in Houston, Texas by Bible Study Media, Inc.

ISBN # 978-1-942243-47-2
Ebook ISBN # 978-1-942243-48-9

Library of Congress Control Number: 2021901103

No part of this publication may be reproduced, stored in retrieval system, or transmitted in any form or by any means electronic, mechanical, photocopy, recording, or otherwise except for brief quotations in printed reviews, without the prior written permission of the publisher. www.biblestudymedia.com.

Unless otherwise indicated, all Scripture quotations are from the ESV® Bible (The Holy Bible, English Standard Version®), copyright © 2001 by Crossway, a publishing ministry of Good News Publishers. Used by permission. All rights reserved.

All Scriptures marked (TPT) are from The Passion Translation®. Copyright © 2017 by BroadStreet Publishing® Group, LLC. thePassionTranslation.com. Used by permission. All rights reserved

Printed in the United States of America.

DEDICATION

I dedicate *Walking in Light: True Life in 1 John* to my three amazing children – Chase, Ashton, and Saxon. My greatest prayer is that you will know the love of God for you, that you will walk in his light and love, and that you will enjoy the assurance of being a child of God. There is no life greater than the life you will find in him and through him. It is truly the Abundant Life – the life that the Lord has for you and the life I long to see you fully embrace and enjoy.

Truly, I love you with all my heart!

TABLE OF CONTENTS

INTRODUCTION 7

DAILY DEVOTIONALS
Week 1 - Real Fellowship 10
Week 2 - Abide in Him 29
Week 3 - Children of God 50
Week 4 - Love One Another 68
Week 5 - God Is Love 88
Week 6 - Child of the Light 106

STUDY GUIDE
Using this Study 127
Outline of Each Session 128

APPENDICES
Frequently Asked Questions 178
Small Group Covenant 182
Group Calendar 183
Prayer & Praise Journal 184
Small Group Roster 185

SMALL GROUP LEADER HELPS
Hosting an Open House 187
Leading for the First Time 188
Leadership Training 101 189

ACKNOWLEDGMENTS 195

INTRODUCTION

After reading and studying this letter from the apostle John, I have realized that I want to be like John. I want his boldness and clarity of thought, but most of all I want his love for God and for God's people. John was a transformed man! Knowing Jesus and living with Jesus changed him from a gruff fisherman to a man who reclined at Jesus' side (John 13:23). Six different times in his writing of the Gospel of John, he referred to himself as the disciple "whom Jesus loved." John knew that Jesus loved him, and John loved Jesus in return. That love for Jesus kept John at his side, all the way to the cross. When every other disciple had fled for his own safety, John stood by the cross and watched while his Savior and beloved friend died.

After Jesus' death, resurrection, and ascension to the Father, John had one passion in life – to make Jesus known. He wanted others to know who Jesus was and what he had done for them. John's Gospel was written for that primary reason. Anyone could read his account and understand that Jesus was God who had come to earth to make the Father known.

John writes this letter to the seven churches in Asia Minor with the same passion; however, this letter to the churches served a different purpose than his Gospel writing. John wrote the Gospel in order for his readers to come to know Jesus, whereas he wrote this letter to people who already knew Jesus. John wanted God's people to live in full assurance of their faith, salvation, and eternal life with the Father. John will take his readers through what has been called a spiral staircase of themes. He starts with the truth, then moves to obedience, and always wraps those two in love. With each twist and turn in John's letter, he will take us deeper into the teachings of Jesus and the love of Jesus.

John's letter was intended to build up his readers to see their faith strengthened in every way. They were facing new challenges in their faith communities. New teachings about Jesus were arising within the church, and these new teachings did not align with what John saw, taught, and wrote. John reminded his readers that Jesus warned that these things would happen. Jesus frequently told of the false teachers who would come among them; these were the wolves in sheep's clothing (Matthew 7:15). John wanted his readers to use the discernment given to them by the Holy Spirit to discern between the true and false teachings so that they would stand firm in their faith.

This disciple whom Jesus loved was well advanced in age as he wrote these words. In fact, he was the last living of the twelve disciples. All the others had already been martyred for their faith. With his age and experience, John knew the challenges his church members faced. John wrote this letter with all the love and tenderness of a doting father, yet he also filled it with boldness and clarity.. John exemplified what it means to speak the truth in love.

John knew and believed with all his heart, mind, soul, and strength that Jesus was the incarnate Son of God who came to offer his life as the perfect sacrifice for sin. John knew the truth, and John would spend every last breath to share the truth and love of Jesus with others.

My prayer through this study is that we will embrace our identities as "the ones whom Jesus loves" and that we would be strengthened in the truth so that we may also proclaim and live that truth out faithfully in this broken world that so desperately needs to see the light of Jesus Christ.

Let's walk in the light together and see what he has planned!

Brooke Hart

DAILY
DEVOTIONALS

WEEK 1
REAL FELLOWSHIP

DAY 1

> *"That which was from the beginning, which we have heard, which we have seen with our eyes, which we looked upon and have touched with our hands, concerning the word of life — the life was made manifest, and we have seen it, and testify to it and proclaim to you the eternal life, which was with the Father and was made manifest to us."*
> **1 JOHN 1:1-2**

TRANSFORMED BY JESUS

For many of the men in my family, there can be nothing greater than a day out on the water catching fish. Oh, the adventure – the joy of flying through the water in hunt of fish, the thrill of finding the fish, followed by the excitement of reeling in the fish! Somehow, it never seems to get old. Day after day, these guys eagerly head out on the water.

John, the apostle and the writer of this epistle, was much like my husband and family, except John didn't just spend time on the water as a pastime. John had a family business of fishing. This family business was clearly a thriving operation as they had their own boats, nets, and a little crew of fishermen. Life was good for John. Then, there came a man named Jesus. As Jesus walked down the Sea of Galilee, he first spotted Andrew and Simon casting their nets into the sea. Not content to leave these men in their family business, Jesus called them into his family business: *"Follow me, and I will make you fishers of men"* (Matthew 4:19). Matthew told us that they immediately did just that – they left their nets and followed Jesus. Walking on from there, Jesus saw another group of fishermen. James and John, the sons of Zebedee, were out in the boat with their father. Jesus called out to them, and they too left everything and followed Jesus (Matthew 4:21-22). John met Jesus, and everything changed!

As John began this epistle, he didn't start with his story or the typical greeting for a letter in his day. Instead, John wrote about this man Jesus, the Word of Life, the one who was at the very beginning. Jesus was with the Father at the beginning of time and was back with his Father as John wrote this letter. Jesus was God made manifest among his people. And John knew Jesus personally. He saw him, touched him, and heard him. For three years, John spent most of his time with Jesus. And Jesus transformed John from a simple fisherman to a disciple of the living God.

Jesus came to offer eternal life. John found that eternal life – life with the assurance of a future home with the Father but also abundant life in this world (John 10:10). Eternal referred to quality as well as to duration. While John left the life he knew, a good life of fishing with his father and brothers, John found a greater life with Jesus. Now, John wanted his readers to experience that same abundant life in this age and the age to come. This eternal, abundant life is available to us today.

REFLECTION

What impresses you about John's heart and intention in these first two verses of his epistle?

Today we read about how John's life was radically transformed by Jesus. How has your life been transformed by Jesus?

DAY 2

"That which was from the beginning, which we have heard, which we have seen with our eyes, which we looked upon and have touched with our hands, concerning the word of life — the life was made manifest, and we have seen it, and testify to it and proclaim to you the eternal life, which was with the Father and was made manifest to us — that which we have seen and heard we proclaim also to you, so that you too may have fellowship with us; and indeed our fellowship is with the Father and with his Son Jesus Christ."

1 JOHN 1:1-3

FELLOWSHIP WITH US

The fellowship that John shared with Jesus was life-changing for him. In that fellowship, John knew with certainty that he was loved by Jesus. John continued to abide in that love of Jesus. That abiding strengthened John and nourished him to fulfill the calling that the Lord had on his life. As one who saw, touched, and heard Jesus, John had been appointed to then write the canons of Scripture, to build churches, and to take the good news of Jesus to the four corners of the earth. Fellowship was the key to John's ministry — fellowship with the Lord, then fellowship with the Lord's people.

Since John could not have face-to-face fellowship with them at that time, John used his words as a means of nourishing his beloved readers. He reminded them here that the invitation was not just fellowship with him and with each other, but that true fellowship was to be found in their relationship with the Father and his Son, Jesus Christ. Man and woman were created in the image of God and were designed to live in an intimate relationship with God. Just as the Father had perfect intimacy with the Son and the Holy Spirt, so men and women are created to enjoy that intimacy with the triune God.

God wants to do life with his people! He wants that kind of relationship, one in which he is known and enjoyed just as the believer is known and enjoyed. That has always been how God related to his people. In the book of Genesis, God called Abram to know him, then God revealed himself to Abram, and he showed him the plans that he had for Abram's life. Through Abram, God created a nation of people for himself. God called the nation of Israel to be his set-apart people. God loved them and cared for them. When they were enslaved in the nation of Egypt, God saw them, and he rescued them. He led them through the wilderness and brought them into the promised land. There, the Lord provided abundantly for his people, he dwelt among them. God has always loved his people and sought to live in fellowship with them.

God wants fellowship with you! John wrote to awaken his readers to this divine invitation. The God of all creation has made the way for them to have unbroken, intimate fellowship with himself. The way to that fellowship is through his Son. Jesus was not only the manifestation of the Father, but he was also the way to the Father. Eternal life was found in the Son as was perfect fellowship with the triune God. They were not only invited into this fellowship, but they were created for this fellowship. That was eternal life and abundant life here on earth.

Fellowship was and is God's answer to loneliness. We live in a day and age when more means of communication are available to us than ever before, yet our world is facing a pandemic of loneliness. Thanks to the work of people like Brené Brown, we have been more aware about the loneliness that has emerged and how detrimental it is to us. Brené offers many wonderful solutions to this loneliness, and I highly value and commend her work. However, even before this awareness, John knew the propensity of mankind to feel lonely, and the answer is found in Jesus Christ.

In Jesus, we can experience fellowship with the Father and fellowship with one another. Throughout his epistle, John will continue to guide his readers to know how to experience this personal fellowship with God and how that personal relationship will translate into a corporeal relationship with other believers. His intention was to invite you into the fellowship, to make sure you know you are welcome and wanted, and to show you the way to this true life in Christ.

REFLECTION
How are you experiencing fellowship with the Father?

DAY 3

> *"And we are writing these things so that our joy may be complete."*
> **1 JOHN 1:4**

COMPLETE JOY

We all long for joy. We long for joy because we were made for joy. Counselors, magazines, and even many preachers expound on this concept of joy and tell us how we can experience it for ourselves. Advertisers then appeal to us through promises that their products will bring us joy. Whether it is joy in that vacation or joy in losing weight through the new tried-and-true program or joy in driving a new shiny car, there are many promises of joy. Unfortunately, these worldly promises for joy never seem to come to fruition. As soon as you finish vacation, work begins; as soon as you stop paying for the new diet products, the weight comes back; and that new shiny car gets dirty and old far too quickly! The world makes many promises for joy, but the world's promises for joy never seem to last.

When John used the word joy, he wasn't speaking of the world's joy but of the joy of the Lord. John knew and believed that true and lasting joy was found only in a relationship with the Lord. While this is the only time that John used the word "joy" in his letter, joy was an underlying theme that ran throughout the letter. John knew and understood that joy was the fruit of a life in Christ. Of course, John had the best example of joy in Jesus. Jesus lived in the joy of the Lord, and he taught his followers to do the same: *"As the Father has loved me, so have I loved you. Abide in my love. If you keep my commandments, you will abide in my love, just as I have kept my Father's commandments and abide in his love. These things I have spoken to you, that my joy may be in you, and that your joy may be full"* (John 15:9-11).

Jesus wanted his followers to experience the fullness of joy in this life as well as the life to come.

Jesus taught that the way to joy was the way of abiding and obeying. A person was to abide in the love of the Father then to obey the commands of his Father. Abiding led to obeying, and obeying led to abiding, and both led to joy – joy that is full.

Even in his old age, John was filled with joy, and he longed to share that joy with his readers and with all of God's people. He had learned the secret of abiding and obeying. This letter is full of John's admonitions to abide and to obey. Just like Jesus, John wanted people to find the joy of eternal life, the joy of living in fellowship with the triune God. John knew this joy, and he experienced great joy in seeing the kingdom of God established on earth. He wrote the epistle so that his joy would be complete.

You, as a reader of his epistle, were part of his joy. He longed for you to share his joy of fellowship and to share his joy in proclaiming the Word of Life to others.

How do you experience joy? Is your life defined by joy? If you hesitate to answer these questions definitively, John would challenge you to examine your life. Are you living in a personal relationship with the Lord? Are you abiding in the love of the Father? Are you obeying his commandments? Are you fellowshipping with the Lord and with other believers? Are you sharing how the Lord Jesus Christ has changed your life? Joy is the fruit of abiding and obeying.

REFLECTION

Are you experiencing this kind of joy today?

Do you truly believe that Jesus is the source of true joy? If so, what would he have you do to cultivate more joy in your life today?

DAY 4

> *"This is the message we have heard from him and proclaim to you, that God is light, and in him is no darkness at all."*
>
> **1 JOHN 1:5**

GOD IS LIGHT

John put on his spokesperson hat here. He took a moment to remind his readers that these words are not his words; these concepts are not his concepts. They are all directly from the Lord. While John might have been quite trustworthy to these readers, God was much more trustworthy. God's truth was the eternal truth and the truth that led to eternal life.

Think back to the crisis in the church of that day. New teachers had emerged with some very strange ideas about who Jesus was and what Jesus had accomplished on the cross. These teachers claimed to receive a "new" revelation about Jesus or to have had some special experiences with the Lord. There was no way to check the revelation or to verify their experiences. Their words had to be trusted at face value, but these new teachings did not align with the teachings of the apostles.

On the other hand, John and the other apostles had heard the very words of Jesus; they saw him with their own eyes; they looked at him, and they touched him (1 John 1:1). Eleven men were left to testify to who Jesus was and what he had accomplished on the cross, and they were in perfect agreement. There was no variation from the truth with their testimony.

With that understanding, John shared the next part of his message: *"God is light, and in him is no darkness at all."* John was saying that God is holy, holy, holy. He is perfectly pure; there is not a flaw in his character. God is all-knowing. He is all-powerful. He sees all and understands all. God is perfect in every way; he is transcendent over all. God is absolutely glorious in every way! Essentially, John was saying that there is no one and nothing else like God.

As the Israelites traveled through the wilderness, God's presence provided the light for them to walk by night. John would have his readers understand that the light of God is much more powerful than darkness. As John wrote in the beginning of his Gospel: *"The light shines in the darkness, and the darkness has not overcome it"* (John 1:5). God's light is powerful; it illuminates the way for his people; and it provides safety and comfort for his people. Children often use night lights because of their fear in the dark, but the clarity of the light can dispel that fear and bring comfort.

"God is light and in him is no darkness at all." Everything about God is good, pure, holy, and true. He is worthy of full trust and obedience. God's light will contrast with everything else in this world for there is nothing else with such purity. In this world, there is light and there is darkness, and occasionally when things line up just right, there may be an overlap of that light and dark to create a shadow. John wanted to live fully in the light of Jesus Christ. He knew the joy, the safety, and the clarity of living in that light. And until he would take his final breath, John would call others to come into the light.

Amy Grant was my all-time favorite Christian musician for many years. Truth be told, I still love her today. Amy could take the words of Scripture, words that I knew in my head, and apply them to my heart. One of her songs that deeply ministered to me about the light of Christ was "Thy Word":

> *Thy Word is a lamp unto my feet and a light unto my path*
> *When I feel afraid, think I've lost my way,*
> *still you're there right beside me*
> *And nothing will I fear, as long as you are near,*
> *please be near me to the end*
>
> *Thy Word is a lamp unto my feet and a light unto my path*
> *I will not forget, your love for me and yet,*
> *my heart forever is wandering*
> *Jesus be my guide, and hold me to your side,*
> *I will love you to the end*

Thy Word," Amy Grant, (Straight Ahead: Meadowgreen Music Co. / Bug and Bear Music), 1984

As I write those words, I feel the same things I did hearing that song twenty years ago. I feel comfort and hope. I feel assured that God is with me, that he will continue to lead me, that his love is steadfast and secure, and that he is absolutely trustworthy.

Amy beautifully conveyed what John wanted his readers to know: *"God is light, and in him is no darkness at all"* (v. 5). In God is perfect truth, holiness, purity, love, forgiveness, joy, and knowledge. Everything you need in this journey of life can be found in him.

REFLECTION

When you read that God is light, what do you think and feel about God? How could his perfect light bring you peace, comfort, and security today?

DAY 5

"If we say we have fellowship with him while we walk in darkness, we lie and do not practice the truth. But if we walk in the light, as he is in the light, we have fellowship with one another, and the blood of Jesus his Son cleanses us from all sin. If we say we have no sin, we deceive ourselves, and the truth is not in us. If we confess our sins, he is faithful and just to forgive our sins and to cleanse us from all unrighteousness. If we say we have not sinned, we make him a liar, and his word in not in us."

1 JOHN 1:6-10

WALK IN THE LIGHT

God is light, and his light is holy, pure, illuminating, guiding, and perfect in every way. Light is glorious, but light can be overwhelming, even frightening. As children of God, we know that his light shines fully into our lives. He sees everything about us – our thoughts, our secret sins, our hidden wounds, our fears, our failures, our doubts. We can keep nothing hidden from his light. Light calls us to complete honesty with ourselves and with the Lord. What can allow us to stand uncovered before him? Nothing but the blood of Jesus!

Light requires honesty, and fellowship with God requires walking in the light. John challenged those who claimed to have fellowship with God yet wanted to remain in the covering of darkness. Where the blood of Jesus allowed the children of God to stand before the Lord and to be perfectly seen, those in the darkness were still seen, but they were under judgment instead of grace. John wrote about light and darkness in his Gospel as well:

> *"And this is the judgment; the light has come into the world, and people loved the darkness rather than the light because their works were evil. For everyone who does wicked things hates the light and does not come to the light, lest his works should be exposed.*

But whoever does what is true comes to the light, so that it may be clearly seen that his works have been carried out in God." **JOHN 3:19-21**

John exposed the hypocrisy of those who said they knew and loved the Lord but walked in perpetual sin. To love sin was to love darkness, and darkness and God were completely incompatible.

John used such strong imagery to inform his readers and raise their awareness. Not everyone who claimed to be a Christian was a Christian. The people in the church who taught anything other than Jesus Christ as the incarnate Son of God did not know Jesus and did not speak truth. They were walking in darkness. John wanted his readers to see through the facades so that they would not be swayed to the darkness.

While the light can be overwhelming and frightening to anyone, a true child of God knows that no matter what is exposed by God's light, he is secure in God's love and acceptance. A child of God would not be perfect; he would continue to sin. However, a child of God would agree with God about that sin. He would not want it in his life, so he would confess that sin, turn from it, and ask the Lord to forgive his sin through the blood of Jesus. A child of the light lives in a continual pursuit of holiness.

Denial of sin keeps a person in the darkness, while confession of sin allows for forgiveness. The blood of Jesus Christ allows for perfect honesty in a person's life. A child of the light has faith in Jesus as the Son of God who died on the cross to take away his sin. No matter what he has done, the blood of Jesus is sufficient to cover the sin, to forgive him, and to allow perfect reconciliation to the Father.

John would go on to say that no one, even he himself, was without sin. The heavenly Father knows his children perfectly; he knows their frailties and fallenness. He never expects perfection; he expects faith in his Son. Man was made for unbroken fellowship with the Lord, and the Lord provided the way for that fellowship. To walk as a child of the light entails being perfectly seen and known by the Lord, having a faith in Jesus Christ as one's Savior, living a confessional lifestyle that turns from sin, and embracing fellowship with God and God's children. A child of the light no longer fears the revelation of sin for he knows that he stands cleansed and healed through the blood of Jesus. John would offer us the opportunity to come out of hiding, to allow God's light to shine into the deepest facets of our lives, and then to allow for the conviction that leads to repentance. God sent his Son into the world so that you could have eternal and abundant life through him. He sees you, he knows you, and he loves you with a perfect and steadfast love. There is great healing and freedom that comes with walking as a child of the light.

REFLECTION

Can you take some time to get honest before the Lord today, to allow him to search you with his perfect light? If you are under the blood of Jesus, you are perfectly secure to stand before the Lord. He loves you and wants to help you clear away any darkness.

DAY 6

> *"My little children, I am writing these things to you so that you may not sin. But if anyone does sin, we have an advocate with the Father, Jesus Christ the righteous."*
>
> **1 JOHN 2:1**

THAT YOU MAY NOT SIN

A simple paraphrase of John's words here would be: Children of God, stop sinning! Sin is not of God nor of the light, but it is of the darkness. You don't want to be in darkness; you want to be in the light. John wrote strong words but with a tender and loving tone. His use of the phrase *"my little children"* conveyed John's love for these readers. When he spoke hard words, he spoke them from that place of love. This elderly apostle desperately wanted to gain his readers' full attention for the duration of the letter. So, children – John's beloved children and God's beloved children, stop sinning.

Self-esteem has become a buzzword these days. Helicopter parents have stepped into schools and onto sports fields with the demand that no one criticize or redirect their children as it may hurt their self-esteem. John was not nearly as concerned with self-esteem as he was with salvation. He spoke truth that could be hard in order to lead his readers into honest self-examination. That examination is not the end goal; it is examination that leads to confession, repentance, forgiveness, and reconciliation to the Lord. The intention is not to make one feel badly about oneself or to feel like a failure, but rather to move that person into a place of healing and restoration, to move from darkness to light. Because of the blood of Jesus, there is always hope. A child of God is to develop self-worth through this relationship with the Lord. The truth is that they are sinners who have fallen short of the glory of God (Romans 3:23). Yet, the Lord made the way for sinners to be cleansed, healed, and fully redeemed.

What John wanted his readers to understand was that they can live free from the hold of sin. Through the Holy Spirit, they can overcome sin in their lives. While the sinful nature will remain, it does not have to control a believer. The more one grows into the knowledge and love of the Lord, the more one becomes like Jesus. Paul wrote about this transformation in his letter to the Corinthians:

> *"Now the Lord is the Spirit, and where the Spirit of the Lord is, there is freedom. And we all, with unveiled face, beholding the glory of the Lord, are being transformed into the same image from one degree of glory to another. For this comes from the Lord who is the Spirit."* **2 CORINTHIANS 3:17-18**

As we behold the glory of God, we are transformed. Paul likened it to when Moses went up on the mountain to meet with God. When Moses came down from the mountain, his face shone with the glory of God so that he had to put a veil on to cover the glory. Our faces have been unveiled, as we have direct access to the Father through the Son. As we gaze upon him, we are changed from the inside out. Our flesh does not have the control over us that it once did as the Spirit takes control of our lives.

Thankfully, the Lord understands that we are not perfect as Jesus. That is why he sent Jesus to die in our place. Jesus, having made the perfect sacrifice for our sins, stands before the Father advocating for us. When we fail, Jesus covers that failure with his shed blood. Through his blood, the Father sees us as righteous before him. Jesus never leaves us to defend ourselves but stands ready to make our defense before his Father. His righteousness becomes our righteousness as his blood cleanses us, heals us, and restores us to a right relationship with the heavenly Father.

In his letter to the believers in Rome, Paul asked the rhetorical question: *"If God is for us, who can be against us?"* (Romans 8:31). With Jesus on our side, we can never lose. Paul offers us powerfully reassuring words:

> *"No, in all these things we are more than conquerors through him who loved us. For I am sure that neither death nor life, nor angels nor rulers, nor things present nor things to come, nor powers, nor height nor depth, nor anything else in all creation, will be able to separate us from the love of God in Christ Jesus our Lord."*
>
> **ROMANS 8:37-39**

A child of God walking in the light will still sin and fall short of the glory of God, but that child will always be accepted, always be loved, and always be forgiven through Jesus Christ.

The apostle John would call us to turn from any sin in our lives through the empowering work of the Holy Spirit. And then, he would remind us that even in our places of sin, we are cleansed and made perfectly righteous through the blood of Jesus. As children of the light, we are more than conquerors through Christ!

REFLECTION

Are you living as more than a conqueror through Christ? How does the Lord want to encourage your heart today to turn from sin and to allow his love to wash over you?

DAY 7

> *"He is the propitiation for our sins, and not for ours only but also for the sins of the whole world. And by this we know that we have come to know him, if we keep his commandments. Whoever says, 'I know him' but does not keep his commandments is a liar, and the truth is not in him, but whoever keeps his word, in him truly the love of God is perfected. By this we may know that we are in him: whoever says he abides in him ought to walk in the same way in which he walked."*
>
> **1 JOHN 2:2-6**

WALK AS JESUS WALKED

In the 1990s, a movement among Christians re-emerged. It was known as WWJD, which stood for "What Would Jesus Do?" WWJD originated in the late 1800s with Charles Sheldon's book entitled *In His Steps: What Would Jesus Do*. Sheldon reminded his readers of the call to be like Jesus or as John said, *"to walk in the same way in which he walked."* In the 1990s, people further developed this movement through devotional books and the wearing of wrist bands with WWJD on them. In every circumstance of a person's life, he or she was to ask the question, "What would Jesus do?" Jesus lived the perfect life. He never sinned; he always honored his Father; Jesus loved people perfectly. Jesus always spoke the truth in love, but he was also always kind, patient, slow to anger. Jesus exemplified every description of love listed in 1 Corinthians 13. A child of God is to walk as Jesus walked – a high and holy calling!

For those who continue to struggle with their sinful nature, who long to be free but continue to feel the effects of sin (and yes, this is all of us), John's words are there to remind us that while we still struggle, the battle has already been won on our behalf. *"He is the propitiation for our sins."* Because of our fallen nature, even when we diligently seek to be like Jesus, we will fall short of the glory of God. Jesus lived the perfect life that we could never live, and Jesus offered himself as the perfect sacrifice for sin. Jesus was both the perfect man and the Son of God – he alone could offer himself as the spotless Lamb to take away the sins of this world. The blood of Jesus propitiated (satisfied) the holy God's need for justice. Through that blood, we find forgiveness for our sins, but it is not only forgiveness that we find. Through Jesus, we are also given favor with the Lord. When a person puts his faith in the person and work of Jesus Christ, he is fully forgiven of his sin so that when the Father looks down upon that person, he does not see sin. He sees the righteousness of his Son. That is the miracle of the cross; that is the miracle of grace!

So, what are we to do with this freedom? Paul asked the same question in his letter to the Romans: *"What shall we say then? Are we to continue in sin that grace may abound? By no means! How can we who died to sin still live in it?"* (Romans 6:1-2). Grace meets us where we are and accepts us where we are, but does not leave us as we are. The grace of God given through Jesus Christ transforms us. That sin which we once loved, we now despise. The sin that held us captive has now been made to release us. There is still a battle between our flesh nature and our spirit nature; however, we know that through the Holy Spirit we have won and will continue to win that battle. Gratitude is our rightful response to the grace of God. Out of that gratitude and a heart of love, we seek to become more like Jesus. We seek to live holy lives as we come to know his commands and obey his commands. We no longer obey God out of fear but out of love. One of my favorite prayers for myself is "Lord, make me to desire what you desire; make me to love what you love and to love others as you love others." I know that I need his Spirit to change my desires. So often, I am short-sighted. I only see what is right in front of me, and my fleshly desires take hold of me. It is those moments that this prayer becomes even more important. The Lord longs to change our hearts. In Ezekiel, he talked of replacing our hearts of stone with hearts of flesh (Ezekiel 36:26-27). He would do that by putting his Spirit within us. That Spirit would transform our hearts to love him and to love his laws.

When Jesus warned his followers about the influence of the religious leaders of his day, he told them to look at the fruit of their lives. The religious leaders knew all the right things to do and to say. On the outside, they appeared to be very holy. However, the fruit of their lives told another story. Instead of producing the fruit of the kingdom of God – love, joy, peace, patience, kindness, goodness, faithfulness, gentleness, self-control – their lives were filled with pride, selfishness, and greed. They longed for the approval of man and commendation of man above the approval and commendation of the Lord.

John wanted us to know how to produce this fruit and to continually have our lives transformed by the Lord. To do so, John told us to abide in Christ. By abiding in him, we would walk as he walked. To abide means to remain, to stay. John called us to remain in the grace of God through Jesus, to stay in his Word on a daily basis, to rely on the power and presence of the Holy Spirit dwelling within us. Then, we would be empowered to walk like Jesus, to obey the commands, and to produce the fruit of the Holy Spirit.

May we choose to abide in him, to remain with the One who has provided us with everything we need for a victorious life and godliness.

REFLECTION

Are you abiding in the triune God and in his Word?

How does abiding in Christ transform you? How can you go deeper into that transformation?

WEEK 2
ABIDE IN HIM

DAY 8

> "Beloved, I am writing you no new commandment, but a old commandment that you had from the beginning. The old commandment is the word that you have heard. At the same time, it is a new commandment that I am writing to you, which is true in him and in you, because the darkness is passing away and the true light is already shining."
>
> **1 JOHN 2:7-8**

THE NEW (OLD) COMMANDMENT

The focus of last week's study was on knowing the truth of God through the person and work of Jesus Christ. John didn't just want his readers to know the truth but to walk as children of the light. A child of the light was not perfect but was perfectly cleansed through the blood of Jesus. That cleansing allowed him to enjoy fellowship with the Father. John began with the vertical relationship between God and his children because a true relationship with the Lord would naturally translate to the horizontal relationships with the rest of God's children. It wasn't enough to love God; God's people were to love one another!

Previously in the letter, John addressed his readers as "little children." Here, John addressed his readers as "beloved." Transformation began within an individual when he knew that he was perfectly known by God and loved by God. John's use of the term "beloved" implied God's love of the readers followed by John's love for the readers. John would model what he taught, for John had experienced the transformation of love in his own life and was empowered to offer love to others.

John and his brother James had been raised to be strong, tough, and always ready for action. When a village of Samaritans did not receive Jesus as John and James expected them to, the brothers asked Jesus if he wanted them to call down fiery judgement from heaven to consume the village (Luke 9:51-56). This kind of behavior awarded John and James with the nickname "sons of thunder." However, by the time John wrote this epistle, his identity had changed from "son of thunder" to *"the disciple whom Jesus loved"* (John 21:20). Later church fathers would call him "the apostle of love." John had been loved by his Savior, and his life now reflected that love for God and for the children of God.

So, John wrote to them about a new commandment that was really an old commandment. How could a commandment be both old and new? John would have his readers think back to a conversation between Jesus and the lawyer who asked which of the commandments was the greatest.
Jesus responded:

> *"You shall love the Lord your God with all your heart and with all your soul and with all your mind. This is the great and first commandment. And a second is like it: You shall love your neighbor as yourself. On these two commandments depend all the Law and the Prophets."* **MATTHEW 22:37-40**

In this response, Jesus combined Deuteronomy 6:5: *"You shall love the Lord your God with all your heart and with all your soul and with all your might,"* with Leviticus 19:18: *"You shall not take vengeance or bear a grudge against the sons of your own people, but you shall love your neighbor as yourself: I am the Lord."* The commandments of the old covenant were to love God and to love one's neighbors; thus, this was not a new commandment. However, no one had ever been able to fulfill these commands until Jesus. Jesus alone obeyed every detail of the Old Testament law.

As the Messiah sent by God, Jesus fulfilled all the righteous requirements of the old covenant while also ushering in the new covenant. The old covenant of Moses was based on law and works. The new covenant of Jesus was based on grace. Through grace, the child of God was forgiven of his sins and filled with the gift of the Holy Spirit. The Holy Spirit then empowered the child of God to obey the commandments, including the commands to love God and to love others. The old had become new through the Holy Spirit.

As God's people obeyed him, loved him, and loved each other, the kingdom of light was expanding throughout the world, and the darkness was passing away. With each redeemed life, the power of darkness was broken. John longed to see light fully overcome darkness so that the kingdom of God could reign in heaven and on earth. John called his readers to securely know the love of the Father so that they would then become conduits of his love to others.

God's people are far too unloved today. How can we live out this command to love one another? Can we see beyond the things that separate and estrange us from God and one another, and cling to the eternal truths that would unite us?

REFLECTION

If the son of thunder could be transformed into the apostle of love, what could be possible in your life through the abiding work of the Holy Spirit knowing that you too you are the disciple whom Jesus loves?

How can you live out this call to love God and to love others today?

DAY 9

> *"Whoever says he is in the light and hates his brother is still in darkness. Whoever loves his brother abides in the light, and in him there is no cause for stumbling. But whoever hates his brother is in the darkness and walks in the darkness, and does not know where he is going, because the darkness has blinded his eyes."*
>
> **1 JOHN 2:9-11**

A CHILD OF THE LIGHT

The call for honesty and self-examination continued for John's readers. He gave them something to think about: Are you a child of the darkness or a child of the light? Those who love their brothers and sisters are children of the light, and those who hate their brothers and sisters are children of the dark. What one professed held no weight in the matter; love was the determining factor.

John's great desire was to provide his readers with an assurance of faith. To do so, John had to write challenging words. As you read through John's Gospel, the book of Revelation, and his letters, you will notice his clear distinctions: light vs. darkness, love vs. hate, truth vs. lies, and child of God vs. child of the devil. When it comes to the kingdom of God and the kingdom of this world, there simply was no neutral ground.

To be a follower of Jesus meant to love God first then to love your neighbor as yourself (Matthew 22:34-39). Fellowship with God naturally translated into fellowship with God's people. Anyone who claimed to be a Christian but did not love his brother or sister was still in darkness. Because he claimed to be a Christian and yet did not love, his false witness would cause others to stumble. The lack of love would deter people from walking with the Lord; his example would lead others into a misguided darkness.

On the other hand, those who proclaim to be Christians and who live out the call to love others will lead others to the Lord and to a deeper understanding of the Lord. There is no cause for stumbling, as the light of God shines in and through that person. They will not be perfect, but the light overpowers the darkness as the believer seeks to live in obedience to the Lord.

John never said that love would be easy! Jesus' love for us took him to death on a cross. What John would say is that love is a decision not an emotion. All throughout the history of the Church, there have been conflicts between Christians. There have been and always will be those people who are easy to love as well as those people who are "extra grace required." When we choose to obey God and to love those "extra grace required" people, God will give us his eyes to see them and his heart to love them. Instead of just seeing the negative in another, we see what God sees – someone he loves. We may become sensitive to some pain or insecurity in that person. As God loves that person through us, light shines in the darkness and healing can happen – healing in them and healing in us.

God's children have received a supernatural love. Jesus made it very clear how we are to love one another: *"This is my commandment, that you love one another as I have loved you"* (John 15:12). Love as you have been loved by Jesus.

John offers us some challenging words to consider today. Are we living in light or are we living in darkness? No matter how you answer that question, there is hope. The Lord would have you come to him, to be cleansed and healed of all your sin, and to enter a relationship with him. This relationship with the Lord is one of divine love. As you are loved, you will begin to love – to love all his children through his supernatural power.

REFLECTION
Who is the Lord calling you to make the choice to love today?

DAY 10

> "I am writing to you, little children, because your sins are forgiven for his name's sake. I am writing to you, fathers, because you know him who is from the beginning. I am writing to you, young men, because you have overcome the evil one. I write to you, children, because you know the Father. I write to you, fathers, because you know him who is from the beginning. I write to you, young men, because you are strong, and the word of God abides in you, and you have overcome the evil one."
>
> **1 JOHN 2:12-14**

YOU HAVE OVERCOME

John moved from challenger to encourager in this portion of his letter: You are the true children of God! You are the ones who are walking in the light! Rest assured my children, for you have the assurance of eternal life. And then John moved into three different designations for his readers: little children, fathers, and young men. These designations were not pertaining to the physical age of the addressees but their spiritual age. In every church at every time in history, there are members of the church in different stages of their spiritual journey. John wanted every true believer to know that he or she has eternal security. Anyone who has put their trust in Jesus Christ as their Savior has been washed of their sins and is in right standing with the Father and with the Son. Every believer in every stage has been given the gift of the Holy Spirit.

John began this section of his letter writing to little children. His use of "little children" implied those who are still immature in faith and needing to be guided, instructed, and disciplined. As Paul wrote to the Corinthians, this is the believer who is still drinking spiritual milk (See 1 Corinthians 3:1-2). Unlike Paul, John was not reprimanding these children but affirming them. They had experienced forgiveness of sin through faith in Jesus Christ. They did know the Father; they were just young in their faith. God had accepted them through Jesus Christ, and they were already adopted sons and daughters of the Father. While they were fully accepted and loved just as they were, they were going to be called to grow up in the faith. That growth and maturation would happen as they remained in fellowship with the Father, studied his Word, and experienced the fellowship of the Father's family.

The second group that John addressed were those whom he referred to as fathers. These were the spiritually mature believers in the church. They had experienced the challenges of the faith; they knew the deceitfulness of the world and the prince of the world; and they enjoyed a deep communion with the Lord and with his people. These were the men and women who would be called to invest in the little children and the young men. They knew the eternal Word of Life, and standing steadfastly in the truth, they could offer Jesus to others.

Finally, John wrote to the young men. These were the Christians who knew the Lord, walked in his light, and were actively engaged in spiritual warfare. As John said, they were overcoming the evil one and they were becoming strong in the Lord through the Word of the Lord abiding in them. These were those believers who actively chose to put on their spiritual armor every day. They knew the prince of darkness was alive and active in this world. While not fully mature in their faith, they were living as *"more than conquerors"* through Christ (Romans 8:37). They were fighting the spiritual battle and winning.

In our churches today, we have little children, fathers, and young men. These are not just the males within the church but every son and every daughter of the King. While we are all in different places in our spiritual journeys, we all have the assurance of faith and the gift of eternal life with the Father. That assurance rests not on us but on what Jesus has done for us on the cross. It is our proclamation of faith in that work that assures us that we are truly children of the light and walking in it.

Fellowship among the believers is grounded in acceptance and love for one another wherever we are on the path, and so encouraging one another to continue to grow in sanctification and holiness of life. Our calling is to spur one another on just as John did in his letter. We come to Christ just as we are, but we are not meant to stay where we are. As we walk in the light, grow in God's Word, overcome our enemy, and mentor others in obedience to the Lord, we become more like Jesus and we *"walk in the same way in which he walked"* (1 John 2:6).

REFLECTION
Who is the Lord calling you to make the choice to love today?

DAY 11

> *"Do not love the world or the things in the world. If anyone loves the world, the love of the Father is not in him. For all that is in the world – the desires of the flesh and the desires of the eyes and pride of life – is not from the Father but is from the world. And the world is passing away along with its desires, but whoever does the will of God abides forever."*
> **1 JOHN 2:15-17**

DO NOT LOVE THE WORLD

The spiral nature of John's letter continued here as John created a sharp contrast between love for God and love for the world. Love for God and love for his people is holy and pure; it is eternal and leads to real life and joy. Love for the world is antithetical to love for God. To truly grasp John's message here, it is important that we understand what he means by the term "world." In John 3:16 we read, *"For God so loved the world, that he gave his only Son, that whoever believes in him should not perish but have eternal life."* If God loved the world so much that he sent his Son, why are we told not to love the world? In John 3:16, the use of the word "world" expanded the kingdom of God from the nation of Israel to all that nations. Paul, the Jew of all Jews, wrote of God's inclusion: *"Everyone who calls on the name of the Lord will be saved"* (Romans 10:13). Through the death and resurrection of Jesus Christ, salvation was made available to all people and all nations.

When John warned against loving the world, he did not mean to not love people of all nations, races, and creeds. After all, he was the one who loved all people, "the apostle of love." Instead, John was referring to the "evil powers of this world which corrupt and destroy the creatures of God," which a new Christian is to renounce in their baptism (Book of Common Prayer, p. 302). In just three sentences, John uses the term "the world" six different times. Word repetition was a literary tool for emphasis. This world's systems and structures have been corrupted by human sin and have aligned with Satan and his evil forces; the world is part of the darkness. The corrupt powers of this world, the sinful desires of the flesh, and Satan with the spiritual forces of evil, collude and conspire as an unholy trinity. Darkness has always hated the light and would seek to destroy the light. Children of the light beware. The evil forces of the world can be crafty, manipulative, and tempting.

For John it was simple. A person could love the world, or a person could love the Father. Typical to John, there was no neutral ground. Joshua, the great leader called to follow Moses, offered a similar challenge to the nation of Israel: *"Choose this day whom you will serve"* (Joshua 24:15). Joshua reminded the Israelites that they could serve the one true living God, or they could serve the gods of the surrounding nations. They could not serve both. Worship of the Lord was exclusive, as was made clear in the first of the Ten Commandments: *"You shall have no other gods before me"* (Exodus 20:3). Love of other gods and love of things of this world crowd out love for God.

Jesus made it very clear that man cannot serve two masters (Matthew 6:24). While John's words can sound harsh and rigid, they are spoken from love. John wrote this letter to remind his readers that there are two major forces at work – the kingdom of heaven that was ushered in by Jesus Christ and the kingdom of this world that was ushered in by the fall of Adam and Eve in the Garden. In fact, John wrote of the same three temptations that Satan used to cause Eve to partake of the forbidden fruit: desires of the flesh, desires of the eyes, and the pride of life.

> *"So when the woman saw that the tree was good for food, and that it was a delight to the eyes, and that the tree was to be desired to make one wise, she took of its fruit and ate, and she also gave some to her husband who was with her, and he ate."*
> **GENESIS 3:6**

The desire of the flesh is the fallen nature that was handed down to us, the unsanctified desires of our flesh. These can be cravings for things like food, alcohol, and sex. While these things may not be inherently sinful, our desire for them can become sinful – gluttony, alcoholism, and extramarital sex.

The desires of the eyes are those things that look good to us and appeal to our senses. Consider how much money is spent on advertising. Companies invest millions of dollars each year to woo us to buy their products. They look good, sound good, and promise satisfaction, joy, or desired transformation. We can be manipulated by the desire of our eyes and led away from things of the light toward things of the darkness.

Lastly, the pride of life is simply our desire for affirmation and to make a good impression upon others. Again, this can be a healthy and good desire until it consumes us. When we find that we long to impress others before God or when we rely on our earthly wisdom or wealth, we have succumbed to the pride of life.

Sadly, all three of these run rampant in our churches today because we do not like to talk about sin. We want to hear that we are good people, that we do good things, and that God is happy with us and wants us to be happy. What we forget in our pursuit of happiness is that God is much more concerned with our holiness. John's letter beautifully conveyed this truth. It is not because God does not want us to be happy; it is because God knows us, truly knows us, and he knows that holiness leads to true and abiding joy as opposed to temporary feelings of happiness. The things of this world that promise to satisfy are often the very things that lead to our destruction.

John concluded this section with the warning that the world and all its promises are passing away. The people who believe and trust in the world are those who are under the dominion of the evil one; thus, they are also passing away. But God's kingdom, God's promises, and God's children will abide forever. They are secure and will overcome this world.

John affirmed to us that assurance will be found in the love of the Lord. When love of the Lord reigns in your heart, everything else will find its rightful place, and you can experience his supernatural joy in this world and the world to come.

REFLECTION

The Lord would call us all to self-examination. Does the corrupt power of this world have a hold on us? Are we captivated by the desire of our flesh, the desire of our eyes, or the pride of life? Our enemy is crafty and longs to move us away from life in the Spirit to life in the flesh. Through confession and repentance, we can renounce the sinful desires of the flesh and move back into life in the Spirit.

DAY 12

> "Children, it is the last hour, and as you have heard that antichrist is coming, so now many antichrists have come. Therefore we know that it is the last hour. They went out from us, but they were not of us; for if they had been of us, they would have continued with us. But they went out, that it might become plain that they all are not of us."
>
> **1 JOHN 2:18-19**

IT IS THE LAST HOUR

Imagine being on an airplane preparing to fly to your destination. As the plane prepares for takeoff, the flight attendant stands up and gives safety instructions that you have heard hundreds of times. Now imagine that same attendant makes an announcement in the middle of some intense turbulence as you feel the plane sinking quickly and shaking fiercely. At that point, you are much more attuned to what she is saying, and you understand the significance of her words. At this point in John's letter, he wanted his readers to pay attention like their plane was going down. These were not routine words; these were words of life and death. Wake up! Listen closely! We are in the last hour!

In these verses, the apostle John addressed the primary motivation of his letter. His original readers would fully understand the situation in the church. Unfortunately, that situation is not immediately apparent to those of us reading this letter thousands of years later. The church John had planted and nurtured throughout the years had experienced a painful division. From within the community of the church, there arose some false teachers who opposed the Word of Life, eternal life, of which John spoke at the beginning of his letter. John went so far as to say that these false teachers were to be considered antichrists. It is important to denote the distinction John made between the final Antichrist that was coming and the many antichrists that had come. We read about the future Antichrist in the book of Revelation. In his epistles, John referred to the many antichrists that were operating in the church in that present day.

Once again, it is essential to be aware of the tone with which John wrote these strong words. He began by addressing his readers as "children." This term of endearment reminded them of John's heart for them. He loved them and longed to protect them from the attacks of the enemy. John's greatest passion was to see the church continue in faithfulness, faithfulness to the teachings of the Old Testament, the words of Jesus, and the apostolic teachings and writings. Anything that veered from these teachings was not of the truth and would not lead to eternal life. John was behaving as a good shepherd would. He admonished the flock to recognize his voice as the voice of truth, the voice to be trusted, and the voice to obey.

John understood that they were in the last days, meaning that they were living in those days between the death and resurrection of Jesus Christ and his coming again in judgment. Jesus warned his followers that in the last days there would be many false teachers; he referred to them as *"wolves in sheep's clothing"* (Matthew 7:15). These false teachers would seek to lead even the faithful followers astray. In John's time, there was the rise of what would come to be known as heresies (false teachings) that denied either the deity of Christ or the humanity of Christ. One such group was called the Gnostics, who claimed special knowledge (Greek: *gnosis*) and secret revelation from the Lord. While it may have seemed special, their revelation did not align with Scripture and the teaching received from Jesus and the apostles. The false teachings led to some very strange and extreme behaviors of either licentiousness or strict asceticism. The fact that these heretics left the fellowship of the church to follow their own way proved that they were not true Christians.

One of the doctrines of the church was perseverance of the saints. True believers would certainly stumble and fall at times, but they would return and come back into the fold and ultimately endure to the very end. John exhorted those who stayed to understand the error of these false teachers and to recognize the dangers of their teaching. John would go on to urge them to be strong in the truth so that they may never be led astray from eternal life.

While these seem like harsh warnings, they are loving pastoral words. They are words written from a wise, old man who genuinely loved the Lord, loved the church, and longed to see it faithfully preserved for the generations to come. John knew the truth and impressed upon all his readers, including you, to cling to that truth. Jesus was God in the flesh; Jesus was sent by God as the promised Messiah; Jesus spoke the words of God; and Jesus died and was raised again so that those who put their faith in him would have assurance of salvation. Without this truth, there is no life. With this truth, there is not just life but eternal life.

You can just imagine John writing these words with the cry of his heart mirroring the words of Moses in the Old Testament: *"Choose life, that you and your offspring may live"* (Deuteronomy 30:19).

REFLECTION

Where do you see the work of false teachers or antichrists in the church today? Why do you think we as a church are so susceptible to their teachings? What do you do to guard your heart and mind from these wolves in sheep's clothing?

DAY 13

> *"But you have been anointed by the Holy One, and you all have knowledge. I write to you, not because you do not know the truth, but because you know it, and because no lie is of the truth. Who is the liar but he who denies that Jesus is the Christ? This is the antichrist, he who denies the Father and the Son. No one who denies the Son has the Father. Whoever confesses the Son has the Father also."*
>
> **1 JOHN 2:20-23**

ANOINTED BY THE HOLY ONE

In the preceding verses, John wrote to warn the readers of the antichrists among them. These people had been in the church and seemingly in fellowship with God's people; however, though they talked the talk of the Christian and worshipped among the body of Christ, they were not authentic believers, as was evidenced in their departure from the church.

Any time there is a division within a church body, it is painful! Unfortunately, I have witnessed the division, not within my own church but in our denomination. No one remained unscathed through that conflict. With a loving and pastoral tone, John addressed the readers' distress and confusion. John warned those who remained in the fellowship of the church about those who would continue to arise to deny the truths expounded within the pages of Scripture. The times were challenging!

In these verses, John moved from a place of warning and back to a place of affirming. Though his readers did need to be aware of what had happened with those who had departed, John took time to assure them that they did know the truth about God and about his Son, and they had the assurance that comes with knowing the truth. Warren Wiersbe explains the controversy: "False Christians in John's day used two special words to describe their experience: knowledge and unction. They claimed to have a special unction (anointing) from God that gave them a unique knowledge. They were 'illuminated' and therefore living on a much higher level than anybody else."[1]

---

[1] *Warren Wiersbe, Be Real: Turning from Hypocrisy to Truth*, 2nd ed. (Colorado Springs: David C. Cook, 2009) p. 92.

1These "illuminated" ones thought of themselves as enlightened beyond those who stayed in the church and the apostolic teachings about Jesus. They looked down upon those who were not open to this enlightenment and not open to their new ideas.

As we read from the beginning of John's first epistle, the truth of God *"was from the beginning"* (1:1). The writer of Hebrews said it this way, *"Jesus Christ is the same yesterday and today and forever"* (Hebrews 13:8). While a believer can grow in spiritual maturity and thus in his understanding of the Word, the Word of God does not change. These antichrists had distorted the truth and believed a lie. John assured the readers that they were the anointed ones, the set-apart ones. In the Old Testament, anointing oil was used to consecrate the tabernacle and the articles used within the tabernacle. The oil was also used to anoint the priests and later the kings and prophets. This anointing oil designated the tabernacle and those individuals as set apart to God and his holy purposes.

With the death and resurrection of Jesus, John's readers were now the ones anointed by Jesus. They had the Holy Spirit not just on them but in them; thus, they were now the ones who were God's set-apart people for his set-apart purposes. The unction the heretics claimed to experience was a false substitute for the power of the Holy Spirit's work in the believer of Jesus Christ. John wrote about this anointing in his Gospel: *"And when he had said this, he breathed on them and said to them, 'Receive the Holy Spirit'"* (John 20:22). Jesus, the Son of God and the fulfillment of all the Messianic prophecies, was God in the flesh. Those who put their trust in him and his work on the cross are the true recipients of this Holy Spirit.

John wrote so that his readers would not be intimidated by those who claimed special knowledge and power. Instead, we are to stay anchored in our proclamation of faith and anchored in our own anointing. John provided a very simple test as to who walks in truth and who walks in lies. The one who denies Jesus Christ is a liar and an antichrist. The one who denies Jesus has no claim to the Father. The one who confesses that Jesus is the Christ is one who walks in truth; that confession and faith ensure us that we have the Father and, as John would later write, we are children of God.

Once again, there is clarity in John's writing – we have seen light and darkness, love and hatred, holiness and sin, and now truth and error. Despite all their grandiose claims, those who left the church walked in error, while those who remained steadfast in their proclamation of Jesus as the Christ walked in truth. May we also live faithfully in our anointing. The Spirit helps us to discern truth and error just as he did in John's day.

REFLECTION

How do you feel about John's clarity between truth and error? Do you trust and surrender to the illuminating work of the Holy Spirit in your life? You, too, are anointed. You are set apart as God's beloved child and set apart to do his holy work in this world.

DAY 14

"Let what you heard from the beginning abide in you. If what you heard from the beginning abides in you, then you too will abide in the Son and in the Father. And this is the promise that he made to us – eternal life. I write these things to you about those who are trying to deceive you. But the anointing that you received from him abides in you, and you have no need that anyone should teach you. But as his anointing teaches you about everything, and is true, and is no lie – just as it has taught you, abide in him."

1 JOHN 2:24-27

ABIDING IN THE TRUTH

John has assured his readers that they have the anointing of the Holy Spirit, the one promised from Jesus to guide them into all truth. As John prepared to transition in his epistle, he brought this section on fellowship with the Father and fellowship within the church to a close with final admonitions or what John Stott referred to as "safeguards to the faith." [2]

The first admonition or safeguard was to abide in the Word of God. He called them to remain in what they heard from the beginning. John laid out this teaching in the first four verses of his epistle. God's Word is the Word of Life. That Word was perfectly proclaimed and lived by Jesus Christ. Jesus came from the Father, lived a perfectly obedient life unto the Father, and died the death that sinners deserved. Through that death and then his resurrection, all those who believed in him would have life, eternal life. Jesus was God incarnate. Though he was fully man, he was also fully God. Those who believe this truth about Jesus walk in the light and have fellowship with the Father and with the Son; this vertical relationship of the believer with the Father was then demonstrated by love for others. This truth about Jesus will not change. The life, death, and resurrection of Jesus was God's redemptive plan from the very beginning. To deny the Son is to deny the Father.

John admonished his readers to believe this truth that he had faithfully taught and to abide in this truth. Abiding in the truth means to stay or to continue in the truth. It is not something a person does once or twice or even once a week.

---

[2] John R. Stott, *The Letters of John, Tyndale Commentaries*, Vol. 19 (Grand Rapids: Eerdmans, 2009) p. 116

Abiding is a daily, moment by moment decision to stay grounded in the Word of God spoken through the prophets, Jesus Christ, and the apostles. To abide in the Word of God means that one does not add to it or take away from it. The entirety of Scripture is to be taught, believed, and obeyed. There is no picking and choosing. As John would say, it is all or nothing; there is no neutral ground.

For those who believe and put their trust in the Word of God and the person of Jesus Christ, there is the promise of eternal life. To remain in faith is to remain in God and in his Son. To remain in God is to remain in his promises. Those who believe will persevere; they will remain in the truth and in fellowship with God and his people; and they will enjoy the eternal benefits. While the world and its many counterfeit promises will pass away, those who do the will of the Father will abide with him forever. John wanted his readers to know that there were eternal consequences to their choices.

The second safeguard is to abide in the Spirit of God, the true anointing. The antichrists would continue to try to lead the true believers astray from the truth. John admonished them again to recognize their deceit and to remain steadfast in their faith. While the antichrists claimed superior knowledge and understanding, the readers had the true anointing and the true understanding through the indwelling of the Holy Spirit. By remaining in that Spirit, they would overcome the deception and the lies. They would recognize error and be able to cling to truth. Jesus spoke to his disciples about the Spirit of truth:

> *"When the Spirit of truth comes, he will guide you into all the truth, for he will not speak on his own authority, but whatever he hears he will speak, and he will declare to you the things that are to come. He will glorify me, for he will take what is mine and declare it to you. All that the Father has is mine; therefore, I said that he will take what is mine and declare it to you."*
> **JOHN 16:13-15**

As believers, we have the very best teacher living within us. All that we hear proclaimed must be tested by the Scriptures and by the Holy Spirit. If we abide in that Spirit, he will enable us to discern truth and error.

Abide. Abide in the Word of Life. Abide in the truth. Abide in the light. Abide in the anointing. Abide in him. As John wrote to the young men, *"you are strong and the word of God abides in you, and you have overcome the evil one"* (1 John 2:14). Victory comes in abiding. That was true for John's original readers, and it is true today.

REFLECTION

Are you living in these safeguards – abiding in the Word of Life and the anointing of the Holy Spirit? Is there room for more – more knowledge and faith in the Holy Scriptures and more surrendering to the power of the Holy Spirit? Take some time today to get still and to ask the Lord to teach you to abide in him.

WEEK 3
CHILDREN OF GOD

DAY 15

> *"And now, little children, abide in him, so that when he appears we may have confidence and not shrink from him in shame at his coming. If you know that he is righteous, you may be sure that everyone who practices righteousness has been born of him."*
>
> **1 JOHN 2:28-29**

ABIDE IN HIM

Most of us are familiar with the phrase, "Just wait until your father gets home." We either heard it from our mothers, we spoke it to our children, or we are the fathers that are expected to do something once home. I was one of those kids who liked to push the boundaries, so I was often the one waiting until my father got home. Here's the thing – my father is one of the most gentle people I know. While he can speak a stern word when needed, my father was not prone to anger or harsh punishment. I felt safe when my father came home. Even when I experienced his discipline, I knew that my father loved me and was for me. That is exactly what John wanted his readers to feel towards their heavenly Father.

To continue with this fatherly imagery, John again addressed his readers as "little children." Imagine the father who bends down to look directly into the eyes of his son. This posture conveys his love and care for the child but also the importance of his words. From this posture, John instructed his children: *"Abide in him."* At this point in the study, we know that to abide means to stay, to remain in the Lord. John was telling his readers to know the Lord, know all about him, spend time with him, pray to him, and seek to become like him. The Lord wants to live in an intimate relationship with you. He wants you to look forward to seeing him face to face!

Just as the Jewish people had long anticipated the coming of their Messiah, Christians are now eagerly awaiting the second coming of Jesus Christ. Where the first coming of Christ was focused on bringing truth, love, and grace to his people, the second coming will be about final judgment and ultimate salvation. When Jesus takes his rightful throne as king of this world, those who have rejected him will face judgment for their sins. Meanwhile, we who have looked to Jesus for the forgiveness of our sins can stand in full confidence. The penalty for our sins has already been paid. The children of God can greet our long-awaited king with full confidence, assured of his love!

No shame, no guilt, just the righteousness of Jesus Christ. The children of God have been reborn like him – holy, righteous, and without sin. We who have been made like him are to act like him, *"to walk in the same way in which he walked"* (1 John 2:6). Children very often become like their earthly parents for good and for bad. If that is true, then how much more should God's children become like him? In him, there is no darkness. As God's children abide in him, we become more like him; we begin to do the righteous work that Jesus did, and God is seen and glorified through us.

John would ask each of his readers to assess their lives. Are you practicing the righteousness of Jesus Christ? Are you becoming more like him? True assurance comes with a life that is reflecting the life and work of Jesus Christ.

REFLECTION

Are you confidently awaiting the second coming of Jesus Christ? If not, how would the Lord like to encourage you or challenge you today to become more like him?

DAY 16

> *"See what kind of love the Father has given to us, that we should be called children of God; and so we are. The reason why the world does not know us is that it did not know him."*
>
> **1 JOHN 3:1**

CHILDREN OF GOD

In the year 2017, my family made a major transition from Lake Mary, Florida to Houston, Texas. The move was life-changing for all of us! That year was a crazy year not just for us but for everyone in Houston. The week we moved, Hurricane Harvey hit Houston and left behind it many devastating results, but Houston Strong rose to the challenge as the Body of Christ stepped into action. It snowed in Houston not once but twice that year; for transplanted Floridians, that was a wonder! If that wasn't enough, the Astros won the World Series. Celebration erupted all throughout Houston, and everything and everyone was decorated in Astros attire. Truly, it was a challenging, inspiring, and awesome time to live in Houston. We marveled in it all!

John wanted his readers to have that kind of awe, wonder, and sense of celebration not about the World Series or Houston Strong, but about what God has done for his people. In my humble opinion, the ESV version does not fully convey John's enthusiasm. My favorite version of this verse is The Passion Translation: *"Look with wonder at the depth of the Father's marvelous love that he has lavished on us! He has called us and made us his very own beloved children!"* (1 John 3:1, TPT). That sounds more like John – *"look with wonder,"* *"love that has been lavished on us,"* and *"beloved children."* The apostle John wanted his readers to marvel at what had been done for them. God had abundantly, lavishly poured out his love on them so that they were now called his children. After ninety years of living, John knew of no greater honor than to be called a child of God.

How do we know that we are truly loved, that we are the children of God? John would say just look at the cross. During Holy Week, we were invited to remember the crucifixion of Jesus Christ on Good Friday. Our church read the passion of Jesus Christ. It is that brutal reminder of what Jesus went through from the Garden of Gethsemane until breathing his last breath on the cross. Jesus, the only man to ever live a perfect life, was convicted based on false charges, then died the most painful and humiliating death a person could die. Why did it have to be this way? Every Holy Week, we sing "My Song Is Love Unknown," the hauntingly beautiful hymn by Samuel Crossman:

> *My song is love unknown,*
> *My Savior's love to me;*
> *Love to the loveless shown,*
> *That they might lovely be.*
> *O who am I,*
> *That for my sake*
> *My Lord should take*
> *Frail flesh, and die?*
> *He came from His blest throne*
> *Salvation to bestow;*
> *But men made strange, and none*
> *The longed-for Christ would know:*
> *But oh, my Friend,*
> *My Friend indeed,*
> *Who at my need*
> *His life did spend*

God is perfectly holy. Holiness and sin cannot coexist. Love motivated God to send his Son. Love motivated Jesus to live among us and to die the death that we should have died. The cross and resurrection of Jesus perfectly demonstrate the love of God and the holiness of God. Love made the way for us to be in relationship with the Father. If you ever wonder if you are worthy of love, remember what God provided for you through his Son.

The writer of Hebrews said it this way, *"Let us run with endurance the race that is set before us, looking to Jesus, the founder and perfecter of our faith, who for the joy that was set before him endured the cross, despising the shame, and is seated at the right hand of the throne of God"* (Hebrews 12:1-2). What was that joy that was before Jesus? You were that joy; I was that joy. Jesus endured the pain and humiliation so that we could live in a reconciled relationship with the Father.

John wanted his readers to delight in this amazing news of being the object of God's joy. At the same time, John warned them that the world would not celebrate them because they didn't celebrate God's very own Son. Darkness hates the light. This world did not recognize Jesus; they crucified him. Thus, this world will not recognize the glorious status of God's children. Christians are never to look to the world for their affirmation or status; those come directly from being a child of God.

Let us examine ourselves again. Who are you aiming to please – the prince of this world or the heavenly Father? John would remind us that the world is passing away while the Lord and his followers will abide forever (1 John 2:17).

REFLECTION

God has lavished his love upon you; you are his child. How do you receive these truths? John would call you to marvel at what God has done for you, and then to abide in his love. There will be no greater joy in this life than the love of the Father.

DAY 17

"Beloved, we are God's children now, and what we will be has not yet appeared; but we know that when he appears we shall be like him, because we shall see him as he is."

1 JOHN 3:2

WE SHALL BE LIKE HIM

Who are you? Where do you find your identity? In case you struggled to articulate an answer, John provided the answer for you – you are the "beloved." God declares that you are his child, that you are loved, and that you are secure in him. You are the beloved of the Lord and thus you are the beloved of John. John's life had been radically transformed by the love of Jesus; it was how he came to define himself – *"the one whom Jesus loved"* (John 13:23, 19:26, 20:2, 21:7, 21:20). John would want every one of his readers to define themselves that way, too. This is who you are right now; this is who you will always be, but there is even more to come!

As God's child, you have a great inheritance stored up for you. Jesus encouraged his disciples with what was to come: *"Let not your hearts be troubled. Believe in God; believe also in me. In my Father's house are many rooms. If it were not so, would I have told you that I go to prepare a place for you? And if I go and prepare a place for you, I will come again and will take you to myself, that where I am you may be also"* (John 14:1-3). Just imagine a heavenly home built by Jesus! Not only does he prepare an eternal dwelling place for us, but he will take us to that home. He wants to be with us! John had confidence in his eternal home. At ninety years old, I would imagine he was eager to get there. He wanted his readers to share in his anticipation and joy.

Here is where John moved from the definitive to the unknown. Some things of the Lord were a mystery, even to the disciples of Jesus. The eschatological future was certain, but the timing and the details were uncertain. In that uncertainty, John alluded to what was yet to come. At this point, his readers had experienced justification through Jesus Christ: the blood of Christ washed away and covered their sins so that they could be in a relationship with the Father. Their justification led to their sanctification, to their lives being transformed to look more like Jesus. What these readers had not yet experienced was the promised glorification.

Glorification would come when the child of God is loosed from his mortal body and is clothed in his eternal resurrected body. No more pain; no more sickness; no more limitation or aging – *"we shall be like him."* Mortal bodies will be exchanged for eternal bodies that are forever like Christ's. This glorification process is not just about the physical body but also the spirit. With glorification of the believer, there is no more sin and depravity. In glorification, there will only be the purity of Christ.

To see Jesus face to face is the ultimate goal and end of the Christian. As Paul wrote to the Corinthian church, *"What no eye has seen, nor ear heard, nor the heart of man imagined, what God has prepared for those who love him"* (1 Corinthians 2:9). John, like Paul, wanted his readers to imagine full glory, holiness, freedom, satisfaction, and joy but then to marvel that God's plan would far surpass our greatest expectations. Surely, what is ahead is greater than any pain, disappointment, or hindrance we will face in this world!

In the good times and the bad times, John reminded us that God is faithful and that he will finish what he has started. Take heart, persevere, and keep your eyes on the goal of glorification with the Father!

REFLECTION

Consider what you are right now – a beloved child of God. Now consider what you will be when you see Jesus face to face. How does the promise of glorification motivate you to live faithfully today?

DAY 18

"And everyone who thus hopes in him purifies himself as he is pure."
1 JOHN 3:3

THE CERTAINTY OF OUR HOPE

When John used the word "hope," there was a different connotation than what we think of today. Think of all the things that you hope for – sunny days, a vacation, a raise, or for the Astros to win the World Series. These are things that we long to have happen; they would delight us. But when John said, *"hope in him,"* his words did not have the uncertainty that our hope can have today. John has already taken us through the transformation process of justification, sanctification, and glorification. While it was something that John would have his readers look forward to, he assured them that there was certainty in their hope; it wasn't a hope that might or might not happen.

John could speak of this certainty because the hope was grounded in Jesus Christ. Thankfully, the hope was not based on believers getting it all right. Jesus already did that! In verse two of this chapter, John assured his readers that they would become like Jesus; they would have glorified minds, bodies, and spirits. If that was their hope, and they knew that glorification was a guaranteed future, how then should they be living right now? They were to live as Jesus lived, to walk as Jesus walked, and to love as Jesus loved.

Jesus was pure in his being. As followers of Jesus Christ, the apostle John called his readers to a process of purification, to continue to allow the Spirit of the Lord to sanctify our lives so that we could live free from the lure of sin and the consequences of sin. James wrote about this cleansing process: *"Draw near to God, and he will draw near to you. Cleanse your hands, you sinners, and purify your hearts, you double-minded"* (James 4:8). James said to draw near while John said to abide. Both indicated that living in closeness to the Lord was essential to the purification process. Draw near, then cleanse your hands. Allow the light to shine into the darkness of the sin, see the sin, confess the sin, and then turn away from it so that true cleansing and healing can come. James reiterated what John has said: you cannot be in light and darkness. When you see darkness, move out from the sin and return whole-heartedly back to the light.

John wanted to motivate us to see beyond this world, the counterfeit gospel messages, and all that will be fading away so that we can put our hope securely in what Jesus has done. The cross and resurrection of Jesus assure believers that we will be eternally glorified with him. Looking ahead to the promises of the Lord breaks the grip of all worldly attachments and sinful behaviors. Behave as the person you will be in eternity – be pure just as Jesus is pure.

REFLECTION

How would the Lord have you purify yourself today? How does looking ahead to the eternal hope of your glorification propel you to obey?

DAY 19

> *"Everyone who makes a practice of sinning also practices lawlessness; sin is lawlessness. You know that he appeared in order to take away sins, and in him there is no sin. No one who abides in him keeps on sinning; no one who keeps on sinning has either seen him or known him."*
>
> **1 JOHN 3:4-6**

WHAT ARE YOU PRACTICING?

When I went to college, I had absolutely no idea what I was supposed to do with my life; there was no sense of calling or even passion concerning my life's work. While I was good at most subjects in school, I never excelled in one particular area. Somehow, I ended up as an English major. I thought it was much more fun to read literature than to read economics! It was fun, but it was also quite challenging. Everyone in the English department knew of Dr. Nan Morrison. She was the only professor who taught the two required Shakespeare classes, and she was known for destroying many a GPA. Needless to say, I entered her Shakespeare I class with great trepidation. Much to my surprise, the class was amazing. Dr. Morrison had me hanging on to her words and longing to understand the literature. To do so, I knew that I needed help, so I requested a meeting with Dr. Morrison.

Our first visit led to weekly visits. These meetings were always the highlight of my week as I would take a list of questions and then listen to Dr. Morrison expound on Shakespeare's work. The writings of Shakespeare came alive to me, and I made the only A in the Shakespeare class. Dr. Morrison came to believe that I was a great English student, and I desperately wanted to live up to her expectations of me. Therefore, I continued meeting with her and worked even harder in Shakespeare II. My time with Dr. Morrison was transformative for me as a student and as a person. Through the love and nurture of Dr. Morrison, I became a passionate and confident English student.

But John would say that a relationship with God is even greater than a relationship with Dr. Morrison. God is not only brilliant, but God is absolutely perfect in his being:

> *"This is the message we have heard from him and proclaim to you, that God is light, and in him is no darkness at all. If we say we have fellowship with him while we walk in darkness, we lie and do not practice the truth. But if we walk in the light, as he is in the light, we have fellowship with one another, and the blood of Jesus his Son cleanses us from all sin."*
> **1 JOHN 1:5-7**

As we contemplate 1 John 1, we see that light conveys the purity and perfection of God. As light shines into darkness, the things hidden are revealed. God's light becomes the means of purification for those who put their trust in the cleansing blood of Jesus. As children of God are cleansed and purified, they continue to walk in the light and to reflect that light to the world.

However, there are also the children of darkness. These are the ones who continue the practice of sinning. Where light brings healing to the children of God, darkness breeds more sin accompanied with the guilt and shame of that sin. Habits build upon themselves. Just as physical muscles are developed through regular exercise, so are spiritual muscles built through daily practices. John says that to continually practice sin is lawlessness; it is to look at the law of the Lord, to see the sin in one's life, and to intentionally choose to remain in that sin.

John the Baptist, while baptizing people in the Jordan river, saw Jesus walking towards him and said, *"Behold, the Lamb of God, who takes away the sin of the world"* (John 1:29). If Jesus came to take away the sins of his people, why would they continue in those sins? It would be like taking a shower only to walk right back into a mud pit. To love Jesus is to love the light and to hate sin. As Dr. Morrison called out the highest parts of me as a student, even more Jesus calls out the highest parts of his children. As children of the light, we are to renounce all sinful practices and to embrace the glorious attributes of the light – holiness, purity, righteousness, and perfect love.

REFLECTION

Are you walking as a child of the light, allowing the Lord to reveal all sinful practices, thoughts, and behaviors? His light reveals so that he can heal. He longs for you to live free from the painful consequences of sin so that you can enjoy true life with him.

DAY 20

> "Little children, let no one deceive you. Whoever practices righteousness is righteous, as he is righteous. Whoever makes a practice of sinning is of the devil, for the devil has been sinning from the beginning. The reason the Son of God appeared was to destroy the works of the devil."
> **1 JOHN 3:7-8**

DO NOT BE DECEIVED!

John was back on eye level with his children again. He spoke in that loving but firm tone. This is important; hear me and heed my words. Again, John warned about those who sought to deceive these Christians. They had left the church to pursue their own "enlightened" ideas, ideas not supported by Scripture. Again, the false teachers, later to be called Gnostics, were the likely subjects here. They felt that their enlightened understanding and spiritual experiences made them superior to those who remained under the Old Testament and the teachings of the apostles. Practices of these false teachers led either to licentious living in which one could fully gratify the desires of the flesh or to an ascetic form of living in which one had to deny the body at all times and in all ways. John warned his readers not to be deceived by either of these false practices.

Instead, John called them back to a biblical understanding of sin. The practice of sinning was a habitual lifestyle of sin. It was the decision to deny the conviction of the Holy Spirit, to disregard the rules and authority of God, and to choose rebellion against God. John took it a bit further here by alluding to the fact that those who lived in this kind of sin and rebellion against God were not children of God but children of the devil. As John repeatedly said, it was not about what one professed but about how one lived.

John went on to teach about the work of the devil. He may have been thinking of the prophet Isaiah's words:

> *"How you are fallen from heaven, O Day Star, son of Dawn! How you are cut down to the ground, you who laid the nations low! You said in your heart, 'I will ascend to heaven; above the stars of God I will set my throne on high; I will sit on the mount of assembly in the far reaches of the north; I will ascend above the heights of the clouds; I will make myself like the Most High.'"* **ISAIAH 14:12-14**

At his creation, the devil was a servant of the Lord. Instead of delighting in who God made him to be, he rebelled against God and sought to rise above God or to be equal to God. Satan moved from a place of surrender to a place of rebellion. At that point, he fell from the heavenly realms and became the great adversary of the Lord. With the death and resurrection of Jesus, the devil was defeated. Though he is a defeated foe, Satan still reigns as prince of the earth. With the second coming of Jesus, that reign will come to an end, and Satan will be thrown into the lake of fire (See Revelation 20:9-10). There, he will suffer eternal punishment and torment.

For those who do not believe in a literal devil, John had a different understanding. John believed in a literal devil, and he believed that the devil was actively working to destroy the Church and to prevent others from coming to the Lord. Satan would use any willing participant in his evil schemes. He would come against those within the Church; he would distort the truth; and he would appeal to the carnal nature of man. John told his precious children to be aware and be on guard so that they would not be deceived.

The only way to stand firm is to abide. Abide in the one who came to destroy the works of the devil. The Holy Spirit, the one whom Jesus Christ gave to all who believe in him, enables us to overcome the schemes of the devil and to live in obedience to the Lord. Once again, John said it is either God's way or

Satan's way. There is no neutral ground. John longed for us to keep walking in the light of God's truth and love.

REFLECTION

Are you aware of the evil that is at work in the world around you? How can you better abide in Jesus so you can resist evil and walk in the light of the Lord?

DAY 21

> "No one born of God makes a practice of sinning, for God's seed abides in him; and he cannot keep on sinning, because he has been born of God. By this it is evident who are the children of God, and who are the children of the devil: whoever does not practice righteousness is not of God, nor is the one who does not love his brother."
>
> **1 JOHN 3:9-10**

WHAT COMPANY ARE YOU KEEPING?

Watch the company you keep! In one way or another, we have all been challenged by these words. As a parent, I long for my children to surround themselves with good friends who reflect the Christian values in which they have been raised. We all know and understand the basic rules of gravity; if you throw a ball in the air, it will come down and with greater force. Unfortunately, it is much easier to get pulled down than to pull others up. The people with whom we spend our time shape our thoughts and often our behaviors, or as my mom always loved to say, "We become like the people with whom we spend our time." My mother always encouraged me to consider whether the people with whom I spent my time led me to make good choices or choices that I would come to regret.

John was asking his readers to also consider who was shaping their lives and their behavior. According to John, there are two options: God or the devil. As we read yesterday, children of God are those who walk in the light, those who turn from their sin and take on the righteousness of Jesus Christ. John then elaborated here with the idea that God's seed would abide in those children. Seed that abides is seed that grows and eventually produces fruit. The child of God will produce the fruit of the Lord or what Paul called fruit of the Spirit: love, joy, peace, patience, kindness, goodness, faithfulness, gentleness, and self-control (Galatians 5:22-23).

Children of the devil are those who continue in patterns of sin. They know their actions are wrong, and instead of repenting and seeking the forgiveness of God, they continue with these habitual patterns. This sin is rebellion against God and clearly demonstrates that they are not children of God but children of the devil. And here's the thing, John didn't care if they were in church every Sunday! As one of our friends and fellow priests loved to say, "Just because you are in the garage does not make you a car!" John would whole-heartedly agree with that statement. Being in church does not make you a Christian. Instead, being in Jesus Christ makes you a Christian, and you can know that you are in Christ by your righteousness and love.

With whom are you keeping company these days? Who has the loudest voice in your life? Who is reflected in the things you read or watch on TV? Who do your thoughts reflect? Is it the Lord, or is it the devil? Though a child of God will sin, that child will not practice habitual sin. Instead, he will agree with God about sin, confess that sin, and turn from it. A child of the devil will live in deliberate sin and rebellion against God. There are no stepchildren of God! You are either a child of God or a child of Satan.

John challenged us to assess our lives and to see whose seeds we are bearing. This assessment can lead to life or death. For those living as a child of the devil, there is time to turn from him and to turn to the Lord. In him, there is forgiveness of sin and a new life found through the anointing of the Holy Spirit. For those living as a child of God, you can stand confident to live victoriously over sin and the devil.

REFLECTION

How is God calling you to make changes in your life to better reflect your heavenly Father?

DAY 22

> *"For this is the message that you have heard from the beginning, that we should love one another."*
>
> **1 JOHN 3:11**

LOVE ONE ANOTHER

Round and round we go! As we are now about halfway through John's epistle, we are aware of the three main themes: truth, obedience, and love. The pattern of John's writing was to hit one theme, transition to the next two themes, then circle back to each one again. It is what the commentators have referred to as the spiral staircase of John's epistle. With each turn, John went deeper in his teaching and had new application. Where one may be tempted to bypass some of John's writing due to the repetition, this spiral teaching challenges the reader to continue to be teachable in the Word of God and to press on to the next level.

This week, we spiral back into the teaching to love one another. This message from the beginning harkens back to chapter two and the old commandment that was also a new commandment (1 John 2:7). It was always God's intention that mankind would love him and love each other. In responding to which was the greatest commandment, Jesus summed up the Old Testament laws: *"You shall love the Lord your God with all your heart and with all your soul and with all your mind. This is the great and first commandment. And a second is like it: You shall love your neighbor as yourself"* (Matthew 22:37-39). These commandments were not new to the church, they were from the very beginning. New came through Jesus Christ and his perfect fulfillment of the law.

Jesus modeled and taught his disciples what this love was to look like:

> *"When he had washed their feet and put on his outer garments and resumed his place, he said to them, 'Do you understand what I have done to you? You call me Teacher and Lord, and you are right, for so I am. If I then, your Lord and Teacher, have washed your feet, you also ought to wash one another's feet. For I have given you an example, that you also should do just as I have done to you."* **JOHN 13:12-15**

Washing feet was the lowliest of the lowly jobs reserved for the lowest servant in the home. In washing his disciples' feet, Jesus taught that to love others was to serve them and to serve them in a self-sacrificial manner.

Jesus broke all the protocols of his day and not just with foot washing. Jesus did not only love those who loved him, but Jesus loved those who betrayed him, falsely accused him, and even crucified him. Some of the very last words of Jesus on the cross were, *"Father, forgive them, for they know not what they do"* (Luke 23:34). Where there had been the teaching of an eye for an eye and a tooth for a tooth, Jesus taught a different way – the way of love and forgiveness. Through the death of Jesus, salvation was available to all people, even those people who nailed him to the cross. There was no limit to the love of God in Jesus!

Throughout his ministry, Jesus exemplified the love of the Father: he fed the multitudes; he touched the untouchables (those considered unclean); he healed the blind, lame, deaf, and even raised the dead. Jesus showed perfect compassion, perfect kindness, and even perfect anger (See Matthew 21:12-13). Unlike the people of his day, Jesus did not just love those who thought like him, behaved like him, or walked in his social circle. In fact, Jesus broadened social circles. He made it a practice to include women in his ministry, to have tax collectors and notorious sinners at his dinner table, and even to speak to Gentiles.

John would have his readers to continue their practice of self-examination. How did their lives demonstrate this love? Were they loving as the world loved, or were they loving as Jesus loved? To walk as a child of God meant to love like Jesus.

What about us? Are we loving like we have been loved by God? The greatest test of love is to meditate on Paul's writing in 1 Corinthians 13:4-7. Each time you see the word love, replace it with your name:

> _____ *is patient and kind;* _____ *does not envy or boast;* _____ *is not arrogant or rude;* _____ *does not insist on one's own way;* _____ *is not irritable or resentful;* _____ *does not rejoice at wrongdoing, but rejoices with the truth.* _____ *bears all things, believes all things, hopes all things, endures all things.*

REFLECTION

Take some time today to replace your name for love. How are you doing? God is not angry at where you fall short, but he longs to help you move more fully into his love so that you may more fully express his love. Spend some time today soaking in his perfect love for you!

DAY 23

> "We should not be like Cain, who was of the evil one and murdered his brother. And why did he murder him? Because his own deeds were evil and his brother's righteous."
>
> **1 JOHN 3:12**

THE LESSON OF CAIN AND ABEL

Every good Jewish person knew the story of Cain and Abel, as it was the account of the first murder in the Bible (Genesis 4:1-16). Parents prayed fervently that their children would not grow up to be like Cain but to be like Abel. Knowing this, John used the example of Cain and Abel to contrast between love and hate, good and evil, children of God and children of the evil one.

A quick recap of this story: Cain and Abel were the children of Adam and Eve. Both men were worshippers of God, and both were called to bring an offering before the Lord. Here is where things got messy. Cain brought an offering from his work – the fruit of the ground. Abel also brought an offering of his work – the firstborn of his flock with the fat offering. The Lord was pleased with Abel's offering but not with Cain's offering. While Abel made his offering in faith, Cain made his offering out of duty and obligation. His heart was not right before the Lord. Surely that would be disappointing, but God told Cain that he can do well; he can make another offering and be right before him. God also warned Cain, *"And if you do not do well, sin is crouching at the door. Its desire is contrary to you, but you must rule over it"* (Genesis 4:7). Here was the decision for Cain: love or hate, good or evil, obey God or obey his evil desires.

Darkness mastered Cain! He was angry at God for refusing his offering, and Cain resented Abel for his righteous deeds. Darkness does not appreciate the exposing nature of the light. Cain resisted the call to repentance and restoration. He would have done well to hear the words of James:

> *"Submit yourselves therefore to God. Resist the devil, and he will flee from you. Draw near to God, and he will draw near to you. Cleanse your hands, you sinners, and purify your hearts, you double-minded. Be wretched and mourn and weep. Let your laughter be turned to mourning and your joy to gloom. Humble yourselves before the Lord, and he will exalt you."*
>
> **JAMES 4:7-10**

The way of the Lord was there and available to Cain. It was the way of humility and repentance; it was to choose to draw near to God to resist evil. Sadly, Cain chose rebellion instead of submission, anger instead of repentance, and Cain's act of murder exposed his heart.

This rebellion, anger, and act of murder clearly demonstrated to whom Cain gave allegiance. Though he had been raised to know the Lord and to love the Lord, Cain was of the evil one. He had been led astray through the desires of the flesh, the eyes, and the pride of life. John alluded to Cain to warn that God's children must guard their hearts and to remember the destructive nature of hate. Paul provided instruction for the child of God struggling with anger: *"Be angry and do not sin; do not let the sun go down on your anger, and give no opportunity to the devil"* (Ephesians 4:26-27). While anger was not sin, what one did with that anger could lead to righteousness or sin.

Anger can become bondage in the life of a believer. As Paul tells us, we should not let the sun go down on our anger, rather we must confess it, turn from it, and ask God to transform our hearts (See Ephesians 4:26). John began this epistle by expressing the desire that his readers would live in the fullness of joy.

Don't be like Cain. Be like Jesus – live in love!

REFLECTION

Are you missing joy in your life because of holding on to anger or hatred? John would have you examine yourself so that you can walk back into the light of God's love, truth, and obedience.

DAY 24

> *"Do not be surprised, brothers, that the world hates you. We know that we have passed out of death into life, because we love the brothers. Whoever does not love abides in death. Everyone who hates his brother is a murderer, and you know that no murderer has eternal life abiding in him."*
>
> **1 JOHN 3:13-15**

CHRISTIAN FELLOWSHIP

Benjamin Franklin is credited with these wise words: "By failing to prepare, you are preparing to fail." That is just what John was trying to do here – adequately prepare his readers for what is to come. *"Do not be surprised"* when the world hates, rejects you, and even crucifies you. John had seen it all through his years of ministry. Remember, he was the last living disciple of Jesus. Every other disciple had been martyred for their faith at the time of this letter.

Just as Cain hated Abel because Abel was righteous, so the world hates those who practice righteousness. Light reveals darkness, and righteousness reveals unrighteousness. If Cain could hate his brother Abel; if Jewish leaders could hate the perfect Son of God; then surely a Christian can expect to be hated by the world. That is the bad news. The good news is that, though hated by the world, Christians who love others have the assurance of eternal life with the Lord. Through their love, they demonstrate a different way in the world, the way of Jesus Christ.

How would the world recognize them as Christians? As the song goes, "They'll know we are Christians by our love." [3] This beautiful song is about Christian unity: being of one Spirit, being restored to one another, working together, and honoring each other. The song exemplifies what John taught throughout his letter. God called Christians to live in fellowship with one another. Fellowship isn't always easy, but as people who abide in the Lord, all things are doable and even enjoyable.

[3] Peter Scholtes, "They'll Know We Are Christians" (1966, F.E.L. Publications, assigned to The Lorenz Corp., 1991)

Again, it was very clear cut to John; the one who loves is of God and the one who hates is like Cain and of the devil. Where love leads to eternal life with the Father, hate leads to death. Just in case John had not been crystal clear, he equivocated hate to murder. John remembered sitting with Jesus and hearing the Sermon on the Mount:

> *"You have heard that it was said to those of old, 'You shall not murder; and whoever murders will be liable to judgment.' But I say to you that everyone who is angry with his brother will be liable to judgment; whoever insults his brother will beliable to the council; and whoever says, 'You fool!' will be liable to the hell of fire."* **MATTHEW 5:21-22**

In this sermon, Jesus took the law and applied it not just to a person's outward behavior but to the disposition of his heart. To be angry at another brother or sister, to hate another brother or sister, was equivocated to murdering a brother or sister.

According to John, the antidote was always to believe in Jesus and to abide in him. One who abides in Jesus abides in the love of Jesus, the grace, and the forgiveness. To not abide in Jesus is to abide in hate and ultimately in death. John would have us check our hearts. Is there any anger hidden there, any resentment, or anything that you need to forgive? Today would be the day to choose the way of love and to allow God's healing to wash over your heart. Festering anger turns to hate, and hate leads to murder. The murderer is not a child of God but a child of the devil. Check your heart!

Before closing, it is important to note that murder is not the unforgivable sin. Instead, it is the ongoing, continual act of anger, hatred, and murder that results in judgment and death. There was and still is time to turn from these sins, to experience the Lord's forgiveness, and to walk into the light of his love and truth.

REFLECTION

Does this teaching seem hard? If so, can you spend some time asking the Lord to soften your heart, to forgive you for harboring anger and hatred, and then to begin the transformation of your heart? He would love to do this work in you!

DAY 25

> *"By this we know love, that he laid down his life for us, and we ought to lay down our lives for the brothers."*
>
> **1 JOHN 3:16**

SACRIFICIAL LOVE

What do you love or profess to love? I love my husband and children; I really love my dog Walter; I love Mexican food, paddle boarding, and the beach. In our society today, we profess love for so many things with very little differentiation of degrees. What does love truly mean, and what kind of love is John speaking of here?

Where John used Cain as the ultimate example of hate and murder, he then used Jesus as the ultimate example of love. Jesus taught his disciples about the nature of love: *"This is my commandment, that you love one another as I have loved you. Greater love has no one than this, that someone lay down his life for his friends"* (John 15:12-13). Jesus did not just talk about love; Jesus demonstrated love in everything that he did all the way to the cross. Jesus gave his very life because he loved his people.

Paul said it this way, *"For while we were still weak, at the right time Christ died for the ungodly. For one will scarcely die for a righteous person – though perhaps for a good person one would dare even to die – but God shows his love for us in that while we were still sinners, Christ died for us"* (Romans 5:6-8). No one did or will deserve the gift offered in Jesus Christ. Despite all that God had done for his people, they continued to sin against him. It was for these unworthy people that Jesus lived and then died. What greater demonstration of love could ever be made?

John does not stop with this ultimate example of love. This demonstration of the love of Jesus was not just to be admired but to be emulated by the followers of Jesus. Jesus laid down his life for us so now we ought to lay down our lives for others. Receive love then give love.

Just prior to his arrest, Jesus shared the Passover meal with his disciples. Even while aware of what laid ahead of him, Jesus loved his disciples and demonstrated that love for them in a very tangible way: *"[Jesus] rose from supper. He laid aside his outer garments, and taking a towel, tied it around his waist"* (John 13:4). Notice that John used the same words here as in our reading for the day – he laid down or laid aside. Jesus laid aside his glory to be made a man; Jesus laid aside his garments so that he could wash the disciples' feet; Jesus laid aside his own desires to obey God and die a sinner's death. Jesus laid it all down for us; we are now called to lay down our pride, our desires, and our comfort to serve our brothers and sisters. After washing their feet, Jesus called his disciples to continue in his example.

Self-sacrifice is antithetical to our human flesh. The flesh wants to protect, prove, and pursue selfish interests. In our flesh, we will not love perfectly or serve perfectly. However, through abiding in the love of Christ, we can experience a transformation of the heart. We can then love those who seem unlovable. What if we were so saturated in the love of God that we asked the Lord to enable us to see that person as he does? Maybe we would see their woundedness, the reality of life in their home, their depression, their fear or anxiety. Maybe if we stopped looking and judging through our own eyes and started seeing and loving through the eyes of Jesus, we could love those we once held in disdain. Instead of judgment, we could feel compassion.

Love transformed John. He went from being called a son of thunder to the beloved disciple to the apostle of love. Jesus saw John in all his sin and yet still chose to put his love upon him. Jesus saw what John was as well as what John could become. Just as love could transform John, love can transform you. He knows your sin; he sees who you truly are, and he sees all that you can be. He lavishes his love and grace on you and then calls you to your own heart transformation. That transformation begins with a request: Lord, I need your help. I have not loved as you have called me to love. Help me to see others through your eyes and help me to love them with your heart. That is a prayer the Father loves to answer!

REFLECTION

Are you willing to surrender your heart unto the Lord, to allow him to create a love in you that is willing to serve sacrificially? Ask the Lord what he wants you to know today.

DAY 26

> *"But if anyone has the world's goods and sees his brother in need, yet closes his heart against him, how does God's love abide in him? Little children, let us not love in word or talk but in deed and in truth."*
>
> **1 JOHN 3:17-18**

THE GOOD SAMARITAN

Yesterday, we looked at the ultimate example of love in Jesus Christ. In everything that Jesus did, he epitomized love. John continued here with the admonition that we are not just to admire Jesus but to emulate Jesus. We are to demonstrate this kind of love to the world. Jesus showed the ultimate love in that he laid down his life for us. While John would not have said that we need to die for others, he did say that we need to love others through our actions and not just our professed words.

As John wrote this, he may have been thinking of the Good Samaritan, the Jewish man who was left for dead on the side of the road by robbers. A priest and Levite walked by him. Maybe they were concerned for the man or even said some prayers for him as they passed right by him; however, they took no action to help the man. By the grace of God, a Samaritan man stopped and didn't only feel concern or offer a prayer. Instead, he bandaged this man's wounds then took him to an inn where he paid the keeper to care for this man. Who would you want to find you on the side of the road? The priest? The Levite? Or the Samaritan man? Who behaved more like Jesus, and who fulfilled the teachings of the Scripture to love God and to love one's brothers?

John would have you ask yourself who the Lord would have you to imitate. John has taught all throughout this epistle that followers of Jesus Christ are to abide in him and in his love. How could one abide in the love of Jesus and receive all those gifts and blessings but not in turn love others? A true believer, a true follower and worshipper of Jesus Christ, will love not just through concern, not just with prayer, but with deeds.

John wanted us to have the full assurance of our faith. Assurance comes through faith in the truth of the Gospel; assurance comes in obedience to the Lord; and assurance comes in loving God and loving the brethren. Again, we look to the example of Cain and his hatred that resulted in the murder of his brother; while Cain presented himself as a worshipper of God, his actions revealed his true nature and his true father, the devil. Jesus loved his brothers and sisters with a perfect love, a love that was willing to make the ultimate sacrifice. The words of Jesus and the actions of Jesus perfectly aligned. Jesus was the incarnate Son of God.

John offered another opportunity for us to assess our lives and consider who we are emulating and who is our true father – the devil or the Lord? Love of the Lord means loving others with a love that sees, stops, and sacrificially serves those in need.

REFLECTION

How are you serving your brothers and sisters in need? Are you one who sees then stops and ministers, or are you one who sees, walks by, and offers up a prayer? How is the Lord calling you to love in action today?

DAY 27

> "By this we shall know that we are of the truth and reassure our heart before him; for whenever our heart condemns us, God is greater than our heart, and he knows everything. Beloved, if our heart does not condemn us, we have confidence before God; and whatever we ask we receive from him, because we keep his commandments and do what pleases him."
>
> **1 JOHN 3:19-22**

BLESSED ASSURANCE

As human beings, we need assurance. We want to see that our money has truly made it into our bank accounts, that our vacation details have been perfectly squared away, and that our appointments have been confirmed. We get receipts, agendas, reminders, and confirmations. Then there are assurances that are not written in ink or sent by e-mail; these may be verbal commitments such as marriage vows or handshakes to seal a business deal.

When John spoke of assurance with the Lord, it was not based on our human standards or a sense of hope. Assurance from the Lord was the only true assurance in this world. While banks, travel agents, personal assistants, and even spouses will fail us in this world, the Lord never will. The assurance we have with him was sealed through the blood of Jesus. When God made a covenant with his people, he was always faithful to that covenant.

"We shall know" was one of John's most frequently used phrases through this epistle. John understood human nature – the doubts, fears, and disappointments that come with earthly promises. John also understood that the enemy sought to undermine a child of God's faith and assurance. Once again, John prepared his readers to stand firm against the deceit of this world and the prince of this world.

Feelings of condemnation assault the children of God. Even the holiest, most devout child of God will not love perfectly. No amount of abiding in God's love can produce perfection in this world. Humans get tired, sick, irritable. That is the reality of life in this fallen world. John assured his readers once again that God does not expect perfection from them. God seeks for his people to experience transformation. Every day is a day to grow stronger and deeper in the love of God and the love for God's people. Perfection will come with glorification. While living and loving imperfectly, the enemy is always there to condemn a person for their shortcomings. While the enemy can taunt, he cannot truly condemn.

Jesus is the way to assurance. When doubts arise, John would have his readers look back to the cross – steadfast love and full assurance of salvation. Jesus not only paid the price for sin, but as we saw in week one, Jesus stands before the Father to always intercede for his children. When the children are weak, Jesus is strong.

The strength of Jesus, the love of Jesus, and the advocacy of Jesus build confidence within believers. God has them and will not let them go. They are his beloved children and inheritors of the kingdom of God. If that isn't enough good news for the day, John wanted his readers to have confidence to approach God in prayer, to make their requests known, and to trust that not only does God hear but that he will answer their prayers. If earthly fathers love to hear their children and grant their requests, how much more does the heavenly Father want to do that for his children? And unlike earthly fathers, the Lord has no limitation in what he can give or do. As David wrote, *"The earth is the Lord's and the fullness thereof, the world and those who dwell therein"* (Psalm 24:1). Everything belongs to the Lord and is under his control.

To come to God in prayer is a demonstration of trust by the child. God welcomes his children; he listens attentively, and he actively works on their behalf. Prayer allows for intimate conversation and relationship. As the children spend time with their Father, they become more like him. They come to love the things he loves, to desire the things he desires, and to do the things he would have them to do. Not only does the Father want to work on behalf of his children, but the children want to work on behalf of their Father. Hence, these precious sons and daughters keep the commandments and do what pleases their Father.

Love begins with the Lord, captivates your heart, then transforms your heart to love God and then to love the rest of his children. The commandments to love God and to love your neighbors are fulfilled in this transformation. God is at work and he will continue to work until each and every one of his children are in their eternal homes with him. Assurance comes with entrusting yourself fully to your perfect heavenly Father.

REFLECTION

How would John want to encourage you in your faith walk today?
When faced with doubts, can you look to the cross of Jesus Christ?

DAY 28

> *"And this is his commandment, that we believe in the name of his Son Jesus Christ and love one another, just as he has commanded us. Whoever keeps his commandments abides in God, and God in him. And by this we know that he abides in us, by the Spirit whom he has given us."*
>
> **1 JOHN 3:23-24**

THE GREATEST GIFT

I love gifts! I love to give gifts, and I really, really love to receive gifts. Clearly, gifts are high on my list of love languages. A thoughtful gift conveys love to me more than words or acts of service. God also loves to give gifts! In fact, the Lord is the greatest gift giver ever! To receive his gifts, one must only believe in his Son. When a person professes faith in Jesus Christ, not only is that person accepted and forgiven, but he is also given the Holy Spirit to live within him. The Lord knew that external words and assurances were great, but that internal words and assurances were even greater.

When divinity lives within the heart of a person, there is new life and new power. What he could not do in his own flesh, he can now do through the Spirit. Paul wrote about this amazing gift: *"If the Spirit of him who raised Jesus from the dead dwells in you, he who raised Christ Jesus from the dead will also give life to your mortal bodies through his Spirit who dwells in you"* (Romans 8:11). If you ever lack your ability to follow through on the commands or directions of the Lord, consider who is in you – the same Spirit that raised Jesus from the dead! What can he not do in you; what can you not do through him?

God, as the greatest gift giver, wanted not only for his children to abide in him but for him to abide in his children. He gave the Holy Spirit as a guarantee, a deposit for all that was to come. With the presence and work of the Spirit, the child of God could fully enjoy the assurance of his faith. Remember why John wrote this letter: *"And we are writing these things so that our joy may be complete"*

(1 John 1:4). John knew that joy came through faith, faith was built through obedience, and obedience was demonstrated by love. All these things happened through the work of the Holy Spirit. John's heart was for God's people to know and experience the fullness of joy, the abundant life that Jesus came to bring (John 10:10).

What more could the Father do on our behalf? He gave us salvation through his Son, the guarantee of eternal life, then the Holy Spirit who secured the deal. Abide in him and he will abide in you – strength for today and hope for tomorrow!

REFLECTION

The same Spirit that raised Jesus from the dead now lives in you. Can you spend some time to ponder this divine gift and mystery? Are you living in the power of this Spirit?

DAY 29

> *"Beloved, do not believe every spirit, but test the spirits to see whether they are from God, for many false prophets have gone out into the world. By this you know the Spirit of God: every spirit that confesses that Jesus Christ has come in the flesh is from God, and every spirit that does not confess Jesus is not from God. This is the spirit of the antichrist, which you heard was coming and now is in the world already."*
>
> **1 JOHN 4:1-3**

TEST THE SPIRITS

While last week ended with great assurance for the true believer, this week begins with another stern warning from John. In essence, John told his readers not to be gullible and listen to "every spirit." John had already addressed the issue of these antichrists in chapter two. John's original audience, the seven churches of Asia Minor, were in a time of turmoil and confusion. Their church had an influx of false teachers; these false teachers professed to be Christians, but they left the fellowship of the church, claiming to have a new and special knowledge of the Lord.

Once again, John began this tough section of his letter addressing his readers as "beloved." When John used that term, he wanted his readers to understand that they were the beloved people of the Lord as well as the beloved people of John. Love motivated John to write tough words. He was deeply concerned for the hearts of his beloved people and these church splits deeply grieved John. Those that had left were bereft of the promises of God. In resisting the right doctrinal teachings of Jesus and the apostles, they had become antichrists, those who opposed the Messiah. Instead of being brothers and sisters in fellowship with Christ and the church, they were now the enemies of God and a threat to the church.

With full awareness of this challenging dynamic, John wrote to his beloved church members and issued two strong commands: Do not believe every spirit and test the spirits. John appreciated that God's people love unity; they were drawn together based on the proclamation of the Lord. What John wanted them to understand was that there was the Holy Spirit who had come from God and there were spirits in this world that were not of God; these were evil spirits, and their goal was to lead the children of God into wrong thinking.

The false teaching that John sought to dismantle throughout this letter was that Jesus was not fully man. The heretical teachings of that day claimed that all flesh was evil and only the spirit was good. They could not accept that Jesus could be fully man and fully God. To deny the incarnation of Jesus Christ was to deny the saving work of Jesus Christ. Jesus came as a man not born by the natural union of a man and woman but of the Holy Spirit. Thus, Jesus could be in the flesh but without the fallen nature of man. Jesus experienced every temptation yet remained without sin. Because he lived a perfect life, Jesus could offer himself as the spotless Lamb, the perfect sacrifice for sin. The incarnation of Jesus, the death of Jesus on the cross, and the resurrection of Jesus are the foundations for the Christian faith and cannot be undermined in any way.

That was John's test for a true Christian – to believe and confess that Jesus Christ has come in the flesh. If there was any deviation from this belief and confession, readers should beware because these are not true children of God; these are antichrists. Do not be naïve regarding the deception of these teachers! John wanted his readers to be confident in the truth espoused by the apostles. This confidence in the truth would allow the true believers to easily recognize variations from that truth. It is much like those who are trained to recognize counterfeit bills. They don't study countless types of counterfeit money, but rather they master the attributes of the genuine and authentic currency.

Throughout the earthly ministry of Jesus, evil spirits recognized him and even called him by name: *"And whenever the unclean spirits saw him, they fell down before him and cried out, 'You are the Son of God'"* (Mark 3:11). Evil spirits know Jesus, but they do not follow Jesus. John would have his readers understand the reality of the spiritual forces in this world. Paul warned of this spiritual battle in his letter to the Ephesians:

> *"Put on the whole armor of God, that you may be able to stand against the schemes of the devil. For we do not wrestle against flesh and blood, but against the rulers, against the authorities, against the cosmic powers over this present darkness, against the spiritual forces of evil in the heavenly places."*
>
> **EPHESIANS 6:11-12**

Christians live in a spiritual battle and must be wise and on guard. Ultimately, Jesus has defeated Satan and the forces of evil. When Jesus comes back to reign on earth, their hold of this world will be completely broken, and they will face judgment. However, until that day comes, there will be spiritual battle between the children of God and the children of the devil.

As John said, *"Beloved, do not believe every spirit, but test the spirits to see whether they are from God"* (4:1). Do not be misled; do not fall away from the Holy Spirit and all the promises of living in a relationship to Jesus Christ. Be wise. Be on guard. Not everyone who professes to be with us is truly for us. Know the truth so that you can discern the lies. John wanted every reader to enjoy the assurance and peace that comes with walking in the light of the truth!

REFLECTION

Just as John warned his original readers, so he warns you today. Are you operating in this awareness? Are you equipped to fight this spiritual battle and to remain steadfast in your proclamation of faith in Jesus Christ as the Son of God?

DAY 30

> "Little children, you are from God and have overcome them, for he who is in you is greater than he who is in the world. They are from the world; therefore they speak from the world, and the world listens to them. We are from God. Whoever knows God listens to us; whoever is not from God does not listen to us. By this we know the Spirit of truth and the spirit of error."
>
> 1 JOHN 4:4-6

HE WHO IS IN YOU IS GREATER THAN HE WHO IS IN THE WORLD

In his fatherly tone and affection, John again addresses his audience as little children. John's stern tone has been replaced by his affirming and assuring tone. Those who sought to deceive these true believers had failed. Hallelujah! John's precious children had overcome the test, had overcome the false teachers, and had chosen to remain in the truth. Their assurance was followed by their affirmation – you are truly children of God! John was absolutely delighted in them. These faithful readers implemented all that John had taught them. They were abiding in the truth, in the light, in obedience, and in love. Through this abiding, they had overcome the works of the enemy and the strongholds of the world.

Affirmation and assurance continued as John reminded them that Jesus was greater than the world. As children of God, they had that greater power living within them through the Holy Spirit. Just as Jesus overcame Satan, death, and sin through his death and resurrection, so now his children had that power to overcome Satan, death, and sin. That was the essence of Christian hope – not only was there ultimate victory in eternal life with the Father, but there was victory to be experienced in this world. Those who departed the church claimed victory through their special revelation and experience; however, it was those who stayed that were the true victors in this world and the world to come. John was one proud spiritual father!

John went on to dispel any ongoing confusion about those who remained and those who left through his Johannine distinctions. Those who left the church were of the world meaning that they were children of the devil. While that may have sounded harsh, these people rejected the apostolic teaching. John and the other disciples had been chosen by Jesus Christ to write the canons of Scripture and to teach the truth of God. Those who received their teaching received Jesus; those who rejected their teaching rejected Jesus.

"We are from God" (v. 6). Those who listened to John and the apostles listened to the very truth of God. Jesus described those who would hear and receive his teachings and those who would not: *"The works that I do in my Father's name bear witness about me, but you do not believe because you are not among my sheep. My sheep hear my voice, and I know them, and they follow me. I give them eternal life, and they will never perish, and no one will snatch them out of my hand"* (John 10:25-28). Be the sheep; listen to the voice of Jesus and follow him. Jesus alone has the gift of eternal life.

As we have seen all throughout John's epistle, there is no middle ground. John affirms those who remain faithful to the apostolic teachings about Jesus and his plan of salvation. While the way to the Father is an exclusive way, every faithful believer is on the way as a true child of God. Having the guarantee of eternal life and the present power of God's Spirit, we are overcoming this world!

REFLECTION

Are you living as one who has overcome the world? What would John say to you today about your faith? Would he affirm you or challenge you to abide in the truth of God revealed through the Scriptures?

DAY 31

"Beloved, let us love one another, for love is from God, and whoever loves has been born of God and knows God. Anyone who does not love does not know God, because God is love. In this the love of God was made manifest among us, that God sent his only Son into the world, so that we might live through him. In this is love, not that we have loved God but that he loved us and sent his Son to be the propitiation for our sins."

1 JOHN 4:7-10

THE ONE WHOM JESUS LOVES

John circled back for the third time in this epistle to the topic of love. What better way to transition to love than speaking of his love for the readers? John's use of the term "beloved" declared his own love for them, but more importantly God's love for them. They were God's children. God loved them with a perfect love, a love that when fully received and understood would not just bless them but would transform them. To experience this radical love of God was life-altering. John was the very best example of this. John and his brother James were called "sons of thunder." But as we read in day 17, John gained another name for himself – *"the disciple whom Jesus loved."* Five different times throughout his Gospel writing, John described himself with this designation (John 13:23, 19:26, 20:20, 21:7, 21:20). In the next to last verse of the last chapter, John made it abundantly clear that he was referring to himself with that description. John experienced the love of Jesus personally, then he saw that love demonstrated for him on the cross. That love radically transformed John from a son of thunder to the apostle of love.

John wanted his readers to know that they, too, were the ones loved by Jesus. As they pondered this love of God and soaked it into their very being, they, too, would be radically transformed. Neither John nor his readers deserved this love of the Father. Just as Paul wrote, *"all have sinned and fall short of the glory of God"* (Romans 3:23). But God – God made the way for these sinners to experience his love through his beloved Son. Jesus was made manifest to John so that he could personally testify to the person and work of Jesus. John spoke directly to that person who wondered if anyone found them to be worthy of love. God did. The question then shifted from whether they are worthy to whether they will receive that love and then will they show that love to others?

John has focused much of his letter on differentiating between the children of God and the children of the world. Here again, John challenged his readers to take a good, hard look at themselves: Are you loving God? Are you loving others? This self-examination had dire consequences. To see that one did not love God nor others was to determine that they did not really know God and had not experienced his salvation. John used parallelism in his sentences to drive that point home – the one who loved was born of God; the one who did not love did not know God.

John would challenge his readers to think about how those who left the church behaved. Had they operated in love? Did they leave in love? John would also challenge his readers to consider if they demonstrated this love among themselves. Was there unforgiveness in the body, judgment, gossip, backstabbing, or exclusion?

The Lord has seen each of us at our very worst, and he has chosen to put his love upon us. John would not take lightly our divisions within the body. More importantly, the Lord would not take lightly our divisions. Jesus told his disciples that if they came to bring an offering and realized that there was division between them and another brother or sister, they were to go be reconciled then to come back to make the offering (Matthew 5:24). Jesus taught a supernatural kind of love, a love that can never be realized or extended without the regenerating work of the Holy Spirit.

"For God so loved the world, that he gave his only Son, that whoever believes in him should not perish but have eternal life" (John 3:16). Perfect love originated with the Father. God's love was demonstrated though his Son. Jesus was the propitiation for sin; Jesus satisfied the demand for justice between a holy God and a sinful people. He met the demands of the law; he paid our debt in full; he took the judgment for our sin. Love begins with God. John exhorts us to marvel in this love of the Father, to be transformed by this love of the Father, and then to demonstrate

this love of the Father. Just like the apostle John, do you know that you are "the one whom Jesus loves"?

REFLECTION

Can you take John's self-designation and apply it to yourself – "I am the disciple whom Jesus loves"? How has your life been transformed by this love of God? How would the Lord want to continue that transformation process? Are there people he would have you love, people he would have you to reconcile to, people that he would have you forgive?

DAY 32

> *"Beloved, if God so loved us, we also ought to love one another. No one has ever seen God; if we love one another, God abides in us and his love is perfected in us."*
>
> **1 JOHN 4:11-12**

LOVE MADE PERFECT

God chose to pour out his love upon us even while we were yet sinners. In seeing our helpless condition, the Lord sent his Son to make the atoning sacrifice for our sins. If that wasn't enough, God has not only invited us to live in relationship with him, but he comes to dwell within us through his Holy Spirit. Through the indwelling Holy Spirit, God's children come to know how deeply loved they are by the Father. Being loved by God would naturally transfer to loving one another. The vertical relationship of the love between God and his child translates into a horizontal relationship of love between God's children. That love is our great testimony to the world.

To the reader in the ancient world, this was a revolutionary kind of love. They were only expected to love those who were deemed worthy of love. Likely, these were the people within their social status, their political party, and their realm of interests. That was the way that the world loved. God's love was radically different than the love of the world. God loved those who were unworthy, those who could not help themselves, and those who had absolutely nothing to offer him. Instead of seeking to have his needs met, God met the needs of those whom he loved by sending his Son. This was the kind of love that God called Christians to have for one another – a supernatural kind of love, a love that surpasses worldly expectations and differentiations, and a love that is demonstrated with deeds.

In calling his readers to love one another, John reminded them that the foundation of that love was the love they had so freely received. It was because God loved them in such a radical way that they then could love one another. This love could not be achieved by human effort; this love could only be experienced and expressed through a posture of receiving. To truly love another person, a man or a woman must be loved first by God.

For far too many years, I lived as a Christian legalist. I knew the rules and expectations for a professing Christian: I had my quiet time every day; I attended church every Sunday; and I could say the right words at the right time to sound spiritual. While my outsides appeared spiritually fit, my insides were hollow, broken, and lacking. I knew God with my head, but I did not experience the love of God in my heart. While I wanted to live the Christian faith, to please God, and to love others, I was exhausted because I was trying to do all that through my own power. I was an empty cup trying to pour out the truth and love of God. What I desperately needed was for God to fill my cup. Thankfully, God met me in my brokenness. His love healed me, and he filled my cup through his love, grace, and goodness. Then, I could share the overflow with others. That is what John is saying in these two verses. A Christian must be filled with the love of God so that his or her life of love is an overflow of his love. To give, we must receive.

John loved because he had been loved. As Jesus had taught and mentored him in the faith, now John taught and mentored these beloved readers in the faith. Light continues to shine in the darkness as believers demonstrate the love of Jesus to their families, their neighbors, and those with whom they did business. These may be people who would not walk into church to hear the Gospel message, but they see the Gospel message being lived among them through the way Christians love each other and those in their communities. The love of God was made manifest through Jesus; now, the love of Jesus is to be made manifest through his beloved disciples. The invisible God is made visible through the lives of his followers – what an honor and privilege to be used by God in such a way!

Beloved, as a dear disciple, live in love. In the receiving and the giving, the love of God is made perfect and complete. Sinners saved by grace are uniquely endowed to demonstrate love and grace to others. Light drives out the darkness as the fellowship of believers grows stronger. John again reminds us that none of this is of ourselves but all of it is by the Lord. Abide in God, and God abides in you.

REFLECTION

How are you reflecting the love of God to others? Do people hear Jesus in your words, see Jesus in your actions, and understand Jesus through your love? How could your demonstration of his love become more complete?

DAY 33

> "By this we know that we abide in him and he in us, because he has given us of his Spirit. And we have seen and testify that the Father has sent his Son to be the Savior of the world. Whoever confesses that Jesus is the Son of God, God abides in him, and he in God. So we have come to know and to believe the love that God has for us. God is love, and whoever abides in love abides in God, and God abides in him."
>
> **1 JOHN 4:13-16**

THE DWELLING PLACE OF GOD

God's true children are now the dwelling place of God. They not only abide in God, but God abides in them. This statement was miraculous to those who received it. As God's chosen people, the Israelites had the presence of God dwelling among them in the tabernacle and ultimately the temple. Then, Jesus brought the presence of God among man through his being, and then he promised to remain with the disciples even after he ascended to the Father. How could Jesus be in heaven with the Father and on earth with his disciples?

Therein lies the great mystery and gift for the child of God. John the Baptist told the people that after him came a greater baptism – a baptism of the Holy Spirit. John's baptism of water was for the washing away of sins; it was an external baptism. What came with the person and work of Jesus was an internal baptism – not just a washing of sins but a filling with the Spirit. The same Spirit that lived in Jesus would now come to live within his followers. In preparation for his death, Jesus told his disciples of the coming Spirit: *"But because I have said these things to you, sorrow has filled your heart. Nevertheless, I tell you the truth; it is to your advantage that I go away, for if I do not go away, the Helper will not come to you. But if I go, I will send him to you"* (John 16:6-7). This Helper would not just live with them but would live in them; he would take the external teachings of Jesus and appropriate them into the believers' hearts and minds. Through this Helper, the followers of Jesus would experience new life and new power.

Sure enough, on the Day of Pentecost, Jesus did pour out the Holy Spirit. John, the other disciples, and all who were gathered were transformed by this coming. Peter moved from denying Jesus three times to boldly proclaiming the truth about Jesus to everyone present; he would go on to speak with that boldness to the religious and political leaders. This once fearful man became the rock Jesus called him to be. His zeal and commitment were so great that he was later crucified for his faith.

These disciples became the powerful disciples Jesus had called them to be. They taught, preached, healed the sick, cast out demons, and built the church of Christ. Now, John exhorts us to become powerhouses for God. How would you do that? Only through abiding. You can have full assurance of your faith through abiding in God, and you come to know and believe God's love for you through his abiding in you. The external words of God's love are paired with the internal presence of God's love. To abide in God is to abide in love and to have love abide in you. What perfect assurance – God in you!

REFLECTION

You are now the dwelling place of the Holy Spirit. Your life is now a reflection of God's truth and love – what a high and holy calling! Can you take some time to abide in him as he abides in you?

DAY 34

> *"By this is love perfected with us, so that we may have confidence for the day of judgment, because as he is so also are we in this world. There is no fear in love, but perfect love casts out fear. For fear has to do with punishment, and whoever fears has not been perfected in love."*
>
> **1 JOHN 4:17-18**

PERFECT LOVE CASTS OUT FEAR

My name is Brooke, and I am a recovering perfectionist. Everything in my being longs to be perfect. I want to be the perfect wife, the perfect mother, the perfect teacher and writer, the perfect friend and daughter. And wouldn't it be great to have the perfect body, the perfect diet, perfect skin, and perfect hair? Every day the media bombards us with images of perfection. If that weren't enough, there is social media there to remind us of all the supposedly perfect people out there. Somehow, they have achieved what we can never seem to attain.

Perfection on our terms will always be unattainable in this world; however, perfection on Jesus' terms is available to us today. If John didn't have our attention before, he certainly has it now as he speaks of perfect love and the casting out of fear. John wanted his readers' full attention here. The children of God are made perfect through Jesus Christ. That is the greatest news ever! No more striving, performing, or comparing. Through faith in Jesus Christ, the child of God is washed of all sins and made perfectly clean, perfectly holy before God. When the Father looks down upon that child, he does not see sin but rather the righteousness of his Son.

The holiness of Jesus is imputed to you as a believer. As Paul wrote, *"Therefore, if anyone is in Christ, he is a new creation. The old has passed away; behold, the new has come"* (2 Corinthians 5:17). In other words, the believer is made perfect through Jesus. While still living in the flesh and still struggling with temptation and falling into sin, the blood of Jesus always washes you clean. No sin can be brought against you.

The child of God is made perfect through Jesus Christ which provides further assurance and confidence before the Lord. John has emphasized the assurance theme throughout the letter, and here he takes the assurance to a new level.

Child of God, you can confidently look forward to the day of judgment for there is nothing to fear. The full payment for your sins has already been paid by Jesus Christ. He took all your sins upon himself. His blood covers those sins so you can stand before the Father without any fear of condemnation. In fact, your judgment was already executed on Calvary.

Jesus took the punishment that we deserve, and we receive the righteousness that only he deserves. As my husband loves to say, we are the spoiled children of God as we have been given everything!

For you recovering perfectionists, maybe it is time to release your regrets, frustrations, and failures unto the Lord so that you can fully receive the perfect righteousness of Christ. Jesus lived a perfect life because he knew you would never be able to do it on your own.

REFLECTION
Are you being perfected in love? How can this love cast out the fear in your life?

DAY 35

"We love because he first loved us. If anyone says, 'I love God,' and hates his brother, he is a liar; for he who does not love his brother whom he has seen cannot love God whom he has not seen. And this commandment we have from him: whoever loves God must also love his brother."

1 JOHN 4:19-21

WE LOVE BECAUSE HE FIRST LOVED US

In yesterday's portion of Scripture, John exhorted us to recognize that perfect love casts out fear. In this section, John reminded his readers of the origin of that perfect love. Love originated with God. God loves sinners. Based on that love, he enacted a rescue mission through his Son, Jesus Christ. Perfect love was demonstrated on the cross.

In today's Scripture passage, we learn another aspect of perfect love. Perfect love not only casts out fear, but perfect love also casts out hate. Pay attention to John's bold proclamation here. John clearly stated that if someone claims to love God but hates his brother, he is a liar. A person's life speaks louder than their words. Anyone can claim to love God but not everyone will obey the commands of God, especially the command to love one another.

John was unapologetically saying that a true child of God cannot hate his brother. Hate is a work of the flesh and an indicator that one is a child of the devil, not of a child of God. John not only exposed hatred as a work of the darkness, but he also called out hypocrisy. In ancient times, they understood the use of the word hypocrite quite well. A hypocrite was an actor on a stage. He hid behind a mask to effectively portray a different reality than his own. In the church, hypocrisy abounds.

John's greatest concern was the hypocrisy of the false teachers. They acted as if they were very devout children of the Lord while they propagated false teachings about the Son of God. These false teachers, or antichrists as John liked to call them, were not living in truth nor in love. Their teachings, their behavior, and their lack of love provided clear evidence that they were not among God's true children.

John would further develop the command to love one another by adding some Johannine logical questioning. How can a person love the God whom he has not seen when he is not loving God's people whom he can see? John is referencing back to the presence of the Holy Spirit within God's children. God's children are the dwelling place of the Lord. They are representatives of God himself. How can a person claim to love God but hate God's dwelling place? That is impossible!

Just in case we missed the commandment, John circles back again. God's children are not just to receive God's love but to be transformed by his love. That transformative work of the Holy Spirit enables them to love God's children. Love is the work of God! In the life of a believer, love often begins with a choice – the choice to obey God. Loving others is not always easy. There have been and always will always be those people who are difficult to love. These are the people who don't vote for our preferred candidates, don't worship as we do, don't observe our rules, or don't carry themselves as we think is appropriate. John would have us know that God loves those people, that God accepts those people, and that God even delights in those people. Who are we to hate what God loves?

To hate another believer is to disobey God and to move out of his marvelous light. Allow the Holy Spirit to search your heart. Imagine the old beloved disciple John bending down to get eye to eye with you. He asks you, "Have you harbored anger and hate toward another brother or sister?" If so, today is the day to turn to the Lord, to confess your unwillingness or inability to love, and to ask the Holy Spirit to transform your heart through God's perfect love.

REFLECTION

Spend some honest time with the Lord. Ask him to search your heart, to reveal any bondage of anger or hatred so that you can repent and fully return to him. He loves you and wants you to have the full assurance of which John writes in this epistle.

WEEK 6
CHILD OF THE LIGHT

DAY 36

> "Everyone who believes that Jesus is the Christ has been born of God, and everyone who loves the Father loves whoever has been born of him. By this we know that we love the children of God, when we love God and obey his commandments. For this is the love of God, that we keep his commandments. And his commandments are not burdensome."
>
> **1 JOHN 5:1-3**

LIKE FATHER, LIKE SON

As I read this passage for today, I think of the phrase, "Like father, like son." Just as a physical son is born with the hereditary traits of his earthly parents, so are the children of God reborn into the traits of their heavenly Father. This leads to a challenging question: who are the children of God? According to the verbiage of our day, we are all the children of God. Can you remember the song, "Jesus Loves the Little Children"? The lyrics of the song are powerful to dismantle racism and to create an understanding that all people are made in the image of God. But, are all people children of God?

Throughout this letter, John has provided three tests to determine if one truly is a child of God: the test of faith, the test of love, and the test of obedience. Faith was defined as an unwavering belief in the incarnate Son of God. Love was defined by God and was perfectly demonstrated on the cross; a believer lives in God's love, then loves God's children. Obedience was defined by keeping God's commandments. If anyone claimed to be a Christian and yet did not profess this truth about Jesus, did not love God's people, and did not obey God's commands, that person was a liar! Profession of faith must be matched by authentic life expression! The children of God would walk as Jesus had walked.

If you pass these tests, John is delighted to say that you are born of God. In the church, we often hear the term "born again" Christians. This term can be confusing to those outside the faith and even to some within the faith.

Nicodemus was also confused about this terminology. Nicodemus was a Pharisee who came to learn about Jesus secretly; he longed to understand who Jesus was and how he demonstrated God's power so remarkably. Jesus explained to Nicodemus that one must be born again to see and understand the kingdom of God. This response led to the infamous question of how a grown man could be born again. Jesus responded, *"Truly, truly, I say to you, unless one is born of water and the Spirit, he cannot enter the kingdom of God. That which is born of the flesh is flesh, and that which is born of the Spirit is spirit"* (John 3:5-6). Jesus wanted Nicodemus to understand that though a man could not physically be born again, he must be born again spiritually. The knowledge and understanding that Nicodemus sought could only be found in the spiritual rebirth that would happen through faith in Jesus Christ as the incarnate Son of God. That faith is outwardly demonstrated through the waters of baptism, then internally experienced in the gift of the Holy Spirit.

A child of God is one who has faith in the incarnate Son of God. Faith is essential to new birth; love for God and love for his children are the natural expression of new birth. In human families, love begins with the father and the mother. Their love brings forth the fruit of children. Those children are loved within the family, and they in turn come to love their parents and their siblings. The same is true for God's family. A child of God is loved first and foremost by his Father. That love is reciprocated and then moves to his brothers and sisters. Once a child has learned to love God and his family, then he can learn to love those outside of his spiritual family. This is the call to evangelism – to go out into the world and proclaim the good news of the Gospel. To effectively speak truth, one must be motivated by love – love for God and love for people.

Faith, love, obedience. To love God and to love God's children requires you to obey the Lord's commandments. Earlier in the study, we considered how the first four of the Ten Commandments were about our vertical relationship to the Father, and the last six commandments were about our horizontal relationship to others. Love for the Father and love for his children will naturally incline you to keep the commandments from your heart. Keeping the commandments of God is the outflow of love and the assurance that you truly are a child of God.

John reminds his readers that the commandments are not a burden or oppressive in any way to the child of God. God is not a killjoy, but rather he is a God who sent his Son to lead his children into abundant life (John 10:10). Love is always the motivation to keep the commandments. Love is a choice, a choice that involves sacrifice. Jesus washed the disciples' feet before his betrayal, then he told his disciples to love one another: *"A new commandment I give to you, that you love one another: just as I have loved you, you also are to love one another. By this all people will know that you are my disciples, if you have love for one another"* (John 13:34-35). Jesus exemplified this love by sacrificing himself on the cross for the forgiveness of the sins of others. His children are now to love each other sacrificially.

Jesus taught that his yoke was easy, and his burden was light (Matthew 11:30). The ways of Jesus contrasted with the ways of the religious leaders in his time. They were notorious for laying heavy burdens on their people.

John told his readers that *"perfect love casts out fear"* (4:18). The life and death of Jesus is about freedom – freedom from the demands of the law, freedom from the bondage of sin, death, and Satan, and freedom from the fear of judgment. As John wrapped up his letter, he called us to come close again, to listen attentively, and to remember who we are – the children of God. Since that is who we are, John would call us to live appropriately, to live faithfully, to live authentically before the Lord.

REFLECTION

Are you living as a "born again" child of God? Has the Spirit washed you and made you new? If so, are you delighting in the love of the Father and the love of his children? John would have you to fully embrace the freedom and joy of your identity. Ask the Lord to lead you more fully into that freedom and joy today.

DAY 37

> *"For everyone who has been born of God overcomes the world. And this is the victory that has overcome the world — our faith. Who is it that overcomes the world except the one who believes that Jesus is the Son of God?"*
>
> **1 JOHN 5:4-5**

OUR VICTORY IN CHRIST

I am the mother to two precious boys and one amazing daughter. Needless to say, with boys in my home, we had a lot of experience with superheroes. We had many adventures with Buzz Lightyear. He was the great hero of the Toy Story series. Buzz Lightyear's most famous words were, "To infinity, and beyond!" Buzz and his team of toys would go on rescue missions. The goal was to keep all the toys together and safe in Andy's room. With all the mischief of dogs, sisters, and the chaos of a young family, this was no small feat. After Buzz, there was Spiderman, Batman, and Superman. We loved and appreciated them all. Every movie, no matter how many times we had seen it, created that sense of fear and then relief as the superhero saved the day. Everyone wants a victory just like everyone wants to be a victor.

While we love these movies and all that they represent, we understand that they are pretend heroes and merely stories. Thankfully, as children of God, we have a real-life hero as well as a historical and reliable story. In these two passages of Scripture, John told us about our very own victory. Just like the superheroes, we have overcome the forces of evil in this world. In the world, evil appears to be triumphant. Yet, the children of God have won! John encourages us to cling to this truth.

Just before his betrayal, Jesus spoke these words to encourage his disciples: *"I have said these things to you, that in me you may have peace. In the world you will have tribulation. But take heart; I have overcome the world"* (John 16:33). Jesus knew that with his arrest and crucifixion, it would appear that he had been defeated by this world and its corrupt leaders. However, Jesus knew the whole story; he knew how it would end. What these leaders did not know or understand was that they were instruments of the Lord to work out his plan of salvation. Jesus overcame the systems of this world, and he is now empowering his children to do the same. The children of God are the overcomers; the children of God live in victory; or as Paul said, the children of God *"are more than conquerors"* through Christ (Romans 8:37).

Three times John used the word "overcome." He clearly wants us to grasp what we have been given in our new birth. John longed to see the beloved children of God behave like victors. The Holy Spirit has been given to God's children as an assurance that they belong to the Father but also to empower them for daily living and daily victory. In addition, the commandments of the Lord are not a burden because the Holy Spirit working in and through the believer makes them a delight. Through the prophet Jeremiah, the Lord foretold of this new covenant: *"For this is the covenant that I will make with the house of Israel after those days, declares the Lord: I will put my law within them, and I will write it on their hearts. And I will be their God and they shall be my people"* (Jeremiah 31:33). Children of God have new hearts that are empowered and equipped to love and to obey. It is not about trying harder but about surrendering to the power within us.

If you are familiar with superheroes, then you will likely know of the Justice League. In the Justice League, individual heroes band together to fight the forces of evil. It is no longer just Superman or Batman. In the League, there are also Green Lantern, Flash, Wonder Woman, Aquaman, and Martian Manhunter. These heroes were powerful on their own, but imagine their power together. If that was true of the make-believe superhero world, how much more true would it be for God's kingdom!

Power is found through the work of Jesus Christ distributed to the children of God in the Holy Spirit. Each child must stay close to his Father, stay in his Word, and obey his instructions. But just think of the power of God's children coming together to share in his victory. The church is to be a league of united triumph over evil, not a place of fear or defeat.

REFLECTION

In these challenging days, are you living as an overcomer through Christ? How could you band together with your brothers and sisters to give and receive encouragement in this truth?

DAY 38

> *"This is he who came by water and blood—Jesus Christ; not by the water only but by the water and the blood. And the Spirit is the one who testifies, because the Spirit is the truth. For there are three that testify: the Spirit and the water and the blood; and these three agree."*
> **1 JOHN 5:6-8**

THREE TESTIMONIES

For modern day readers, it is helpful if we remember the reason John wrote his epistle. Heresies were arising in the church. In fact, there had been what one might have called a separation of the church much like we have seen in our day. The difference here, though, is that those who left were what John referred to as antichrists or false teachers. These people did not leave because of disagreements in how to do liturgy, the role of women, or even matters of sexuality. These people left the church because they disagreed with John and the other apostles concerning the incarnate Son of God.

Church splits are always painful, but especially when the departing group claims to have a superior knowledge over the remaining group. The heretical teachers of John's day considered themselves to be enlightened with new understanding and revelation about Jesus. This new revelation did not line up with previous revelation; thus, these new teachers elevated themselves above the apostles and even above Jesus Christ as they denied the fundamental statements Jesus made about himself. Instead of God's Word being the truth, these new teachers considered their understanding and their own revelation to be the truth.

To combat this teaching, the apostle John returned to the issue of authority. Who determines truth? Just as love originates with God, so truth originates with God. Turn back to the beginning of John's epistle. Where most letters of that day began with a typical greeting, John bypassed that normal greeting to make an immediate declaration about the Word of Life – the one who was with the Father from the beginning, the one made manifest, the one whom John and the other disciples saw and touched. As an apostle for Jesus Christ, John was commissioned to write Scripture, to teach the Gospel message, and to build up Christ's Church. John knew the truth, spoke the truth, wrote the truth, and lived the truth.

Those who denied these teachings of the apostles were denying Christ himself and proving that they were not children of God but children of the devil. In our Scripture passage for today, John presented the authoritative word about Jesus. The entirety of John's letter centered upon this truth of Jesus Christ. It was not just John and the other disciples that attested to the person and work of Jesus Christ but also the water, the blood, and the Spirit.

In Deuteronomy, God was very clear as to the nature of witnesses to either exonerate or convict a person charged with a crime: *"A single witness shall not suffice against a person for any crime or for any wrong in connection with any offense that he has committed. Only on the evidence of two witnesses or of three witnesses shall a charge be established"* (Deuteronomy 19:15). Whereas the new teachers had no witnesses and just their own experiences and special revelation, John wrote of the validity of witnesses on behalf of Jesus Christ.

Witness number one on behalf of Jesus Christ is the water. All four Gospel writers included the baptism of Jesus, exemplifying the importance of the event. Though John the Baptist resisted the idea of baptizing Jesus, Jesus insisted, *"Let it be so now, for thus it is fitting for us to fulfill all righteousness"* (Matthew 3:15). John was baptizing men and women for the repentance of sin and in preparation for the kingdom of heaven. Unlike any other person whom John had baptized, Jesus had nothing for which to repent. The significance of Jesus' baptism was his identification with sinful man. As Jesus came out of the water, the heavens opened, the Spirit came down like a dove, and the Father's voice from heaven spoke: *"This is my beloved Son, with whom I am well pleased"* (Matthew 3:17). Though Jesus received a baptism of repentance, the Father's voice affirmed his sinless nature. Jesus was declared as the beloved Son of God, the Messiah, the one for which the nation of Israel had been waiting. Through this incarnate Son, the kingdom of heaven had come to earth.

Witness number two on behalf Jesus is the blood. While Jesus' ministry began with his baptism, Jesus' ministry on earth ended with his death on the cross and the words: *"It is finished"* (John 19:30). The salvation of mankind could not be won through the life of Jesus alone. To see a perfect life would be inspiring but also guilt invoking – who else could else could live that kind of life? Salvation required a blood offering. The Hebrews understood this concept well. Since the fall of Adam and Eve, mankind had been making animal sacrifices to atone for their sins. Sin requires atonement. Jesus became that perfect atoning sacrifice on behalf of mankind. The blood of Jesus testified to his humanity while his atoning sacrifice for sin attested to his perfection as the begotten Son of God.

Finally, witness number three is found in the Spirit. Where the water and the blood were external witnesses to Jesus, the Spirit was an internal witness to Jesus. When one is born again through faith in Jesus Christ, the Holy Spirit comes upon that individual, fills him with the presence of God, and attests to the truth of Jesus Christ. The power of the Spirit within does not just enable belief but inspires growth in faith and validates the experience of transformation from the old life to the new life in Christ. John recorded Jesus' teaching about the witness and work of the Holy Spirit in his Gospel: *"When the Spirit of truth comes, he will guide you into all the truth, for he will not speak on his own authority, but whatever he hears he will speak, and he will declare to you the things that are to come. He will glorify me, for he will take what is mine and declare it to you"* (John 16:13-14). The Holy Spirit within the believer is the way God testifies to the truth of who Jesus is and what Jesus has done on behalf of his children.

These are three strong witnesses to the truth of Jesus. John had seen the truth and heard the truth, and now he witnessed to the truth. You must either accept the truth of Jesus to live as a child of God or reject the truth of Jesus and live as a child of the world. The three testimonies provide strong determination of who is born of God and who is born of the world. As John ended his letter, he asked us to consider if we look more and more like our heavenly Father. He reminded us to observe the lives of others. Their walk has to match their talk.

A true child of God does more than say the right words; a true child of God looks like his Father!

REFLECTION

Like father, like son. How would your spouse, your children, your friends, or your parents describe you? Do those descriptions resemble the character of God and his Son, Jesus?

DAY 39

"If we receive the testimony of men, the testimony of God is greater, for this is the testimony of God that he has borne concerning his Son. Whoever believes in the Son of God has the testimony in himself. Whoever does not believe God has made him a liar, because he has not believed in the testimony that God has borne concerning his Son. And this is the testimony, that God gave us eternal life, and this life is in his Son. Whoever has the Son has life; whoever does not have the Son of God does not have life."

1 JOHN 5:9-12

HAVE THE SON, HAVE LIFE

John's straightforward writing style challenged his original readers just as it challenges us today. John was referring to the testimonies of the water, the blood, and the Spirit. These three things together provide an authoritative witness to the person, divinity, and work of Jesus. John now called his readers to consider why they could believe the testimony of other human beings while rejecting the testimony of the infinite God who exemplifies every aspect of truth.

Bring it to our present day. All day, every day, we trust the testimony of people. It may be our financial consultants, doctors, teachers, lawyers, pilots, or even the crazy drivers in the lane next to us on the highway. If we are continually putting our trust in fallible men and women, why do we struggle to trust an infallible God? If the testimony of a fallible human carries weight, consider how much greater weight the testimony of God carries.

Where verses six through nine discuss the testimony, verses ten through twelve discuss the results of that testimony. In perfect Johannine style, he says that the testimony either leads one to believe in the Son or to reject the Son. For the one who believes, the testimony becomes greater through the presence and work of the Holy Spirit. To reject the truth of Jesus Christ is to call God a liar. If you deny Jesus as the incarnate Son of God, deny the testimony of God the Father about his Son, you put yourself above God and say that you understand truth better than God does.

Belief in the Son means eternal life with the Father. *"There is no fear in love, but perfect love casts out fear. For fear has to do with punishment, and whoever fears has not been perfected in love"* (1 John 4:18). If you are a child of God, you need not fear judgment. Jesus has already taken your punishment upon himself. However, if you are a child of the world, you have everything to fear in judgment, for you will be held accountable for every sin, every act of rebellion, and your rejection of God's Son.

Eternal life with the Son or eternal life with the devil. John did not speak in his own authority but spoke in the authority of his Savior. John's words were an echo of Jesus' words: *"I am the way, and the truth, and the life. No one comes to the Father except through me"* (John 14:6). God has made it abundantly clear that the only way to him is through his Son; Jesus has made it abundantly clear that he is the only way to the Father; the Holy Spirit makes it abundantly clear that Jesus is the only way to true life.

REFLECTION

John stated that there is one way to God and that is through his Son. Do you believe this testimony of John? Have you put your trust in the Son? How do you encourage others to do the same?

DAY 40

> *"I write these things to you who believe in the name of the Son of God, that you may know that you have eternal life. And this is the confidence that we have toward him, that if we ask anything according to his will he hears us. And if we know that he hears us in whatever we ask, we know that we have the requests that we have asked of him."*
>
> **1 JOHN 5:13-15**

OUR CONFIDENCE

Verse thirteen ideally would be read on the heels of verse twelve: *"Whoever has the Son has life; whoever does not have the Son of God does not have life. I write these things to you who believe in the name of the Son of God, that you may know that you have eternal life"* (1 John 5:12-13). As John moved towards the end of his letter, he focused back on the purpose for his writing. The apostle of love wanted to encourage and assure his beloved readers that they were indeed the true children of God. These churches had experienced the turmoil of heresy within the church followed by the departure of those who had once been in their church fellowship. For his readers, this was a time of crisis. Those who remained in the church were left with questions and confusion – who were the true followers of Jesus Christ?

John wrote to answer that question. He wanted his readers to know that they were the true church, the true followers of Jesus Christ, and thus the true recipients of eternal life. John combatted all the heretical teachings of his day by reminding them that there is plan A: the way of Jesus Christ, and there is plan B: the way of the world. There is no plan C. Any version of faith that does not proclaim that Jesus is the incarnate Son of God who died on the cross to take away the sin of the world is not of Christ but of the devil. To have the Son is to have eternal life. John wanted his readers to rest in the full assurance that comes with their faith. They had the promise of eternal life; if you recall, John repeatedly made the point that this eternal life is not just in the future, but it can be experienced today.

Eternal life is found in Jesus Christ. John created a connecting bridge here between the opening and closing statements of his letter. In the opening, he said, *"the life was made manifest, and we have seen it, and testify to it and proclaim to you the eternal life"* (1 John 1:2). Jesus Christ, the eternal life, is the way to salvation but also to quality life or abundant life here in this world. Part of that abundant life is the assurance that we, as children of God, can approach him boldly and with great confidence. We are welcome in his presence and our requests are important to him.

As I write this, I can't help but think of the story of Esther and how Mordecai challenged her to go before her husband, the king, to request help on behalf of the Jewish people. Esther knew that approaching the king could result in death. The providence of God made the way for Esther to approach the king and then to save her people. Today through Jesus, the providence of God has made the way for his children to approach the King of all Kings. Not only may we enter, but we may enter with confidence and assurance that the King loves us, wants to hear our requests, and will work on our behalf. In his closing words, John spoke again of the blessed assurance the children of God have – assurance of both eternal life with him and life with him in this world. The Lord offers to us not just the blessings of eternal life but also abundant life with him today.

REFLECTION

How do these assurances speak to your heart? What more would the Lord have you to know of your eternal life and your abundant life in him?

DAY 41

"If anyone sees his brother committing a sin not leading to death, he shall ask, and God will give him life – to those who commit sins that do not lead to death. There is sin that leads to death; I do not say that one should pray for that. All wrongdoing is sin, but there is sin that does not lead to death. We know that everyone who has been born of God does not keep on sinning, but he who was born of God protects him, and the evil one does not touch him. We know that we are from God, and the whole world lies in the power of the evil one."

1 JOHN 5:16-19

PRAYING FOR SINNERS

If you want to clear out a room full of people, bring up the topic of sin. No one likes to talk about sin, especially their own sin. We hide it, deny it, or make excuses for it. Unabashedly, John addressed the issue of sin all throughout his letter. In these last few words from John, we see a new twist in dealing with sin. An aspect of loving the brethren was praying for the brethren, especially in times of sin. These words were new to everyone, but especially to the Jewish readers. For years, the priests and the prophets were the ones who dealt with the sins of the people. Here, John was asking that the lay people take it upon themselves to advocate for their brothers and sisters. Advocacy entailed action, rather than turning a blind eye to their sin. Instead of turning that blind eye, John would have them to recognize the sin and to pray for the person committing the sin. Sin was not to be glossed over but dealt with so that in no way could the believer be hindered in his or her walk with God.

The dualism in John's teaching was again quite apparent as he differentiated between two kinds of sins and the responses to those sins. There is sin that does not lead to death and then sin that does lead to death. John said to intercede for the sin that does not lead to death. These were sins that were observable to the human eye, things that did not align with the Word of God. It could have been flirtations between neighbors, taking an extra head of lettuce from the market, or lying to one of the elders. These things could have been ignored or dismissed. But John understood the gravity of sin, and John understood that Christians need each other in their fight against sin; therefore, encouragement and accountability within the body of Christ is vitally important. Sin is not to be part of the body of Christ, as it robs people of their intimacy with Christ, of their joy, and of the assurance that is rightly theirs in Jesus Christ. As a community, John would have his readers to acknowledge the sin among them and to pray for the sinners so that the bonds of sin could be broken, and believers could live in the abundant life of Jesus Christ.

John loved the body of Christ and loved healthy fellowship within the body of Christ. His heart's passion was to protect the church and to see it thrive. The prince of this world wants nothing more than to destroy the church. What better way to destroy the church than to distort truth, to bring confusion, and to create disharmony among the members? The heretical teachings did just that. The sin which leads to death is the rejection of Jesus Christ, denying Jesus Christ as the incarnate Son of God, denying that Jesus came by water and blood, or any teaching that denies the atoning sacrifice of Jesus Christ. The significance of the atonement is in the fact that Jesus was born a man, lived a perfectly obedient life, then offered himself as the perfect sacrifice for sin. Through his death, Jesus paid the ultimate price for sin so that all who believe in him can find forgiveness of their sin and a reconciled relationship with the Father. John started his letter with this truth and has woven it in throughout the entire fabric of the letter. This truth of Jesus Christ is the way to salvation and the way to live as a child of God. Jesus Christ is not just a way to the Father, but he is the only way to the Father.

John went on to write that the Lord will restore his children when they sin. As he said earlier in his letter, *"My little children, I am writing these things to you so that you may not sin. But if anyone does sin, we have an advocate with the Father, Jesus Christ the righteous. He is the propitiation for our sins"* (1 John 2:1-2). While Christians will continue to struggle with sin and will fall into sin at times, Jesus has made the payment for those sins. The pattern of sin will be broken as the Christian grows into new life, a life that is continually transformed to look more like Jesus.

John wrote that the key to overcoming sin and the devil is to abide in God. John then wrote of another glorious assurance the Christian has in Jesus Christ. Jesus himself will not only advocate for his children before the Father, but

Jesus will protect the child of God from the evil one. In this world, a child of God will face all the temptations of their own flesh, of the evil one, and of the world. If you belong to God, your assurance is that though you may face these temptations and even fall into sin at times, the evil one will never get a permanent hold on you. Jesus spoke these words to his disciples, *"My sheep hear my voice, and I know them, and they follow me. I give them eternal life, and they will never perish, and no one will snatch them out of my hand. My Father, who has given them to me, is greater than all, and no one is able to snatch them out of the Father's hand. I and the Father are one"* (John 10:27-30). The flesh, the evil one, and the world may feel powerful; however, Jesus and his Father are much more powerful. Once you are a child of God, you are always a child of God.

Jesus will not let you go. His Father will not let you go. There is perfect assurance in being a child of God.

REFLECTION

In your struggle with the flesh, the evil one, and the world, how can you find encouragement in the promise that God will not let you go?

DAY 42

"And we know that the Son of God has come and has given us understanding, so that we may know him who is true; and we are in him who is true, in his Son Jesus Christ. He is the true God and eternal life. Little children, keep yourselves from idols."

1 JOHN 5:20-21

KEEP YOURSELVES FROM IDOLS!

The apostle John began his epistle with certainty, and he also ended with certainty. In fact, the phrases "we know," "that we may know," and "you know" occur at least eighteen times throughout this short letter. John wrote that his readers "may know" that they were the true children of God and recipients of his eternal life. John wrote that they "may know" the truth with such certainty that they could recognize any variation from that truth. While many people would not approve of John's black-and-white terminology and his clear distinctions, Jesus had commissioned him to speak this truth. John knew that truth led to eternal life with the Father; thus, truth was of paramount importance to John. Of course, John knew the truth personally. The letter began with the proclamation of knowing the truth in the person of Jesus Christ – the truth that John saw, touched, and now testified to through his writing, teaching, and life. John recorded the words of Jesus in his high priestly prayer: *"And this is eternal life, that they know you, the only true God, and Jesus Christ whom you have sent"* (John 17:3). Eternal life, the true God, and Jesus Christ are intricately woven together, and Jesus Christ has made the way to the only true God and to eternal life. Truth is found in his humanity, his divinity, and his atoning work on the cross.

John's love for his people was clearly expressed throughout his letter. In that love, John sought to protect his children from errant teachings, to ground them in the truth of Jesus Christ, and to assure them of their faith. To do this, John spiraled through three main themes: truth, obedience, and love. A life in

Christ is a life grounded in truth; a life in Christ is demonstrated by walking in obedience to the commands of the Lord; and finally, a life in Christ produces love for God and for God's people. Life in Christ begins with a proclamation of faith in who Jesus is and what he accomplished on the cross for his people. When John wrote his Gospel, it was to share this good news of Jesus Christ so that people would come to believe in him. When John wrote this epistle to the churches in Asia Minor, it was to remind them that they were God's people, they were walking and living in truth, and thus they were true children of the light.

As children of the light, we are to live wholeheartedly before the Lord. Therefore, John concluded the letter with these words: *"Little children, keep yourselves from idols"* (5:21). It wasn't just the heretical teachings that can draw a child of God away from the Lord but also the love of the world. John had already warned his readers about this wrong love of the world, but in his final words, John reiterated that we are to guard our hearts, guard our lives, keep the first things first, and keep Jesus Christ first. There are so many distractions in this life, yet none can offer the true life of Jesus Christ. An idol is just a substitute for the real thing. John would say, do not settle for the substitute but stay focused and committed on what was and still is true.

Jesus was from the beginning and will be to the end. To stay true to him you must abide – abide in him; abide in light; abide in the Word of God; abide in truth; abide in the anointing; abide in God. And here is the promise to you who abide – God will also abide in you. Just as God was made manifest to John, God will make himself manifest to you, his child, through the gift of the Holy Spirit. That Spirit will be the light for you, beloved, as you walk faithfully through this world and into eternal life with the Father.

REFLECTION

Consider how the idols of your life keep you from being fully surrendered and committed to Jesus Christ. How is the Lord calling you to walk as a child of the light today?

USING THIS STUDY
HOW TO GET THE MOST OUT OF THIS STUDY

As with any individual or small group study of God's Word, you largely reap what you sow—or, as it is commonly put, you get out of it what you put into it. But additionally, there are guidelines that can help you get the most from the efforts you put in. I have outlined some suggestions here for you and your group to review before you get started.

1. Review the Table of Contents. The section entitled "Small Group Leader Helps" lays out best practices for how to host and facilitate a healthy small group and avoid common mistakes. It's a great idea to review this material before having your first meeting.

2. This book is a tool for facilitation. Adapt it to the needs of your group. If a line of discussion leads to green pastures outside the scope of the book, enjoy the leading of the Good Shepherd. Feel free to ask, or allow other members to ask, insightful questions as the Holy Spirit leads.

3. There is a lot of material here. You do not have to ask every question in your group discussion. Feel free to skip questions as needed and linger over the ones where there is authentic conversation.

4. Enjoy the experience. Christian community should be characterized by joy and love. Encourage yourself and the group members to bear such fruit. Pray before each session—ask God to minister to you, the facilitator, and every group member by name. Pray for the discussion, the fellowship, and the personal application.

5. Read the "Outline of Each Session" on the following pages so you understand the flow of the session and how the study works.

OUTLINE OF EACH SESSION

OPENING AND CLOSING PRAYER

Begin and end each session with prayer. Invite God into the midst of your conversation. Use the prayers provided or offer one of your own. The prayers provided could be offered by a member of the group or you could all say them together. Close your group with an offer to pray with one another. There is a prayer journal on p.184 where you can keep track of prayer requests and God's answers to your prayers.

KEY VERSE

Each session begins with a key verse. This verse is a key to understanding the entire week's theme. You may want to memorize these verses. By committing portions of God's Word to long-term memory, you will always have them to refer to even when you don't have a Bible with you.

WALKING IN LIGHT

As we gather, a couple of questions are offered to rekindle the fire of our faith in God and mutual commitment to walk in the fellowship of the light. Use the opening questions as an opportunity to reconnect each week and re-engage in the discussion.

WALKING IN TRUTH

Christians leak. As many times as we have heard the truth of God, we need continual reminding. The video teachings and assigned group Scripture reading are there to help us focus on the truth found in the testimony of God's Word.

The video segment will provide teaching on the passage and direction for the session, serving as a launchpad for your discussion. You can watch this video ahead of the meeting as individuals, or if possible, watch it as a group. If you are hosting this group as an online group and are experiencing diminished quality, you may need to encourage members to take time to watch the video on their own rather than try to play it through your online meeting platform.

The "Video Notes" section offers summaries of key points from the video teaching. You may want to ask the group a simple question after the video, something like: "What resonated with you from that video teaching?"

There will also be a section of Scripture for the group to read aloud. Questions will follow to help group members make observations and interpret the text. Use as many or as few of these questions as prove helpful.

The "Study Notes" section provides space to take notes as you watch the video or hear inspirational thoughts from the Lord or members of your group.

WALKING IN LOVE

As we hear God's Word together, we are called to respond by being drawn into deeper love of God and one another. This section of every study will seek to call your hearts to greater intimacy and vulnerability with God and your brothers and sisters in Christ. The questions in this section will invite you to apply what you are learning through fellowship, prayer, and corporate worship.

DAILY DEVOTIONALS

Studying 1 John is like climbing a spiral staircase. With each step, the reader is invited to climb higher into God's truth, light, and love. Set aside time to engage with the Lord each day. The devotionals will stimulate your personal interaction with God and his Word. Pray and ask the Lord to reveal himself to you through the pages of his Word. Use the space provided to journal what you are hearing and learning from the Lord or to express your prayers and praises.

SESSION 1

REAL FELLOWSHIP

"That which we have seen and heard we proclaim also to you, so that you too may have fellowship with us; and indeed our fellowship is with the Father and with his Son Jesus Christ."

1 JOHN 1:3

OPENING PRAYER

Father, it is a great mystery to us that the triune God, the Creator of all that is, wants to have fellowship with us. We are humbled and so deeply grateful. Open our hearts and our minds to hear you, to know you, and to faithfully respond to your invitation. Bless our time of fellowship as we seek you together. In Jesus name. Amen.

QUESTION
What is real authentic fellowship?

SESSION INTRODUCTION

The Apostle John wrote this epistle towards the end of his life. Many believe he was around 90 years of age by the time he wrote this letter. John was the last living disciple who had personally experienced the life and ministry of Jesus Christ. John's beloved friends and fellow apostles had all been martyred for their faith.

John alone was left with his vivid memories and his passion to share the ministry of Jesus Christ that had so radically changed his life. In these last days, John wanted to build up the church and to exhort them to live into the fullness of life in Christ. To know Jesus was to know God. To know God was to know the Word of Life—the source of all life and the source of eternal life.

Eternal life was to be found in Jesus Christ alone. This point was not only fundamental to people coming to salvation but to living as children of the light. Darkness had descended upon the churches in Asia Minor through false teachings about the person and work of Christ. John wrote to assure his readers that the faith handed down to them by John and the apostles was the true faith, the saving faith that led to eternal life.

John called his readers then and his readers today to abide in the truth of Jesus Christ the incarnate Son of God. To abide in truth was to walk in the light and to enjoy fellowship with God and his children.

WALKING IN LIGHT

1. If you are a new group or have new members, take a moment to introduce yourself. Share a hope or expectation you may have for this group and your study of 1 John.

2. Is there a difference between worldly friendship and Christian fellowship? How might you explain?

Watch the Video

The video teaching can be found at **biblestudymedia.com/walkinginlight**. If you are hosting this group as an online group and are experiencing diminished quality, you may need to encourage members to take time to watch the video on their own rather than try to play it through your online meeting platform.

Video Notes

Fellowship in the Truth: John's heart is clearly displayed throughout his epistle. He wrote to dispel any doubt that Jesus was God, came from God, and dwelt among his people as a man. Knowing Jesus is the way to eternal life and true life in this world.

Fellowship in the Light: God is light, and in him no darkness is found. John called us to recognize the divine attributes of the Lord then to allow his light to shine fully into our lives. That light shines so that all the darkness within is overcome, and we may live as God's beloved children.

Fellowship in the Son: John wrote so that we may not sin. Through Jesus Christ, there is freedom from sin and victory over sin in this world. Yet, when we do fail, the words of John remind us that we have an advocate standing before the throne of God. Jesus Christ, the one who made the perfect payment for our sins, never leaves us defenseless.

What resonated with you from this teaching?

WALKING IN TRUTH

Read *1 John 1:1-2:6*.

3. What was John's desire for the people of the church as he expressed it in 1:1-5?

4. What do these verses say is the biggest barrier to real fellowship with God (1:5-10)?

5. What was John conveying about the character of God when he said that *"God is light"* (v.1:5)?

6. John said that Jesus is our advocate with the Father (2:1). How does this help you?

WALKING IN LOVE

7. Discuss the word "propitiation" (2:2). Were you familiar with this word? How do you understand it, and what does it mean for your relationship with God?

8. John called us not only to acknowledge our sin but to confess the sin, turn from it, and receive God's forgiveness and cleansing? Why is it so hard, yet so important to do this? How could you grow in this area?

9. What does it mean to you to have real fellowship with God? What is your vision for deeper fellowship with other Christians?

10. What does it mean for you to abide in him (2:6)? Could you incorporate more of that abiding in your life? Discuss what that would look like and what steps you can take towards walking the same way Jesus walked?

PRAYER REQUESTS

You may want to share prayer requests with one another. There's a Prayer & Praise Journal found on p.184 where you can keep track of your group's requests. Have someone close in prayer or pray the following prayer together:

Father, we long to abide in you, to abide in your Word, and to be led by you. We thank you for the amazing gift of forgiveness through your Son, our Savior Jesus Christ. Teach us to truly dwell in your light throughout this week and bring us back together in the fellowship of your Son next week. To him be the glory. Amen.

STUDY NOTES

STUDY NOTES

SESSION 2

ABIDE IN HIM

"But the anointing that you received from him abides in you, and you have no need that anyone should teach you. But as his anointing teaches you about everything, and is true, and is no lie — just as it has taught you, abide in him."

1 JOHN 2:27

OPENING PRAYER

Come, Lord, and speak to our hearts. Attune our ears to your truth so that we may know you, love you, and walk with you. Teach us to abide in you through your Holy Spirit so that we may know the assurance and joy of your eternal life. Amen.

QUESTION:
What does it mean to abide in the Lord?

SESSION INTRODUCTION

The life of the Christian is one of transformation. That transformation entails moving from darkness to light. The transformation begins with a personal proclamation of faith. As we put our faith in Jesus Christ and his atoning work, we enter into a personal relationship with the Father. As we grow in the love of our Father and our understanding of him and his Word, we will naturally come to love God's people. The Christian faith starts with the vertical relationship to the Father, then expands to a horizontal relationship to the body of Christ.

While there are stages in the Christian journey, the end is the same – eternal life. To experience that eternal life, John calls the believer to abide in the light, to abide in love, to abide in truth, to abide in the anointing of Jesus, and to abide in him. Through this abiding, the believer will be strengthened for every challenge of living in this world.

John wanted his readers to know the many challenges they would face in these last times. He warned about loving the world and the things of the world. John then warned about those who would deny Jesus Christ as the Son of God. The prince of darkness is the prince of this world, and he will seek to lead even the most faithful believers astray. The antidote to the world and the false teaching of the world is to abide in Christ.

WALKING IN LIGHT
1. Do you see the love of God as having transformed your life?

2. While it can be easy to love God, it can be challenging to love God's people. John taught that love for God will expand into love for God's people. How has God been teaching you to love others?

Watch the Video

The video teaching can be found at **biblestudymedia.com/walkinginlight**. If you are hosting this group as an online group and are experiencing diminished quality, you may need to encourage members to take time to watch the video on their own rather than try to play it through your online meeting platform.

Video Notes

Abide in Truth: As we celebrate the Easter season, the apostle John reminds us how the death and resurrection of Jesus Christ has provided a new way for us. In Christ, we are called from darkness to light. To live in the light is to know and love the Father, the Son, and the Holy Spirit.

Abide in Light: John wrote that to abide in the light is to love God and God's children. To not love God's children is to walk in darkness. There is light or darkness; there is love or hate. There is no neutral ground.

Abide in Love: Once someone has walked into the light through faith, transformation begins. Ideally, there is a progression of faith. John writes to people in all stages of faith: little children, fathers, and young men. While all have the assurance of eternal life, there are differentiations between their spiritual maturity. In loving one another, John would have us to encourage each other to grow and mature in faith.

Abide in the Word of Life: John earnestly warns believers to guard themselves against love for the world and against false teachers. While in the world, the Christian must be anchored in the Word of Life to resist the lure of the world and those who would lead them astray.

Abide in Him: True life, eternal life is found through abiding in him. What resonated with you from the video teaching?

WALKING IN TRUTH

Read *1 John 2:7-27*.

3. What are some of the main differences between those who abide in the light and those who remain in darkness (2:7-11)?

4. What spiritual maturity level do you most resonate with and why: children, fathers, young men? Based on that, what does John say to you?

5. *"Do not love the world or the things in the world"* (v. 15). What do you think John meant by "the world"? The things of this world are passing away while the things of God are eternal. John would call us to live with an eternal perspective. Discuss the challenges of living in the world but not being of the world.

6. Discuss the desires of the flesh, the desires of the eyes, and the pride of life. How is the believer called to safeguard against these desires?

WALKING IN LOVE

7. John warned about love of the world but also about the teaching of antichrists within the fellowship of believers. How do you recognize false teaching in the church or those who would lead you astray from the true faith?

8. John spoke of the anointing that every believer receives through the Holy Spirit (2:20). How do you experience this anointing? How does the Holy Spirit help you to discern between light and darkness or truth and lies?

9. John taught that believers are to abide in light, love, the anointing, and in God. What does this practice of abiding look like in your life?

How would the Lord like to take you deeper into this practice of abiding? How can this small group support you?

PRAYER REQUESTS

You may want to share prayer requests with one another. There's a Prayer & Praise Journal found on p.186 where you can keep track of your group's requests. Have someone close in prayer or pray the following prayer together:

Lord, you have called us to abide in you, in your Word, and in your anointing. We ask that you take us deeper into this abiding process and teach us how to support one another, encourage one another, and deepen one another in the Word of Life. Continue to guide us this week that we may gather again in your name and for your glory in the weeks to come. Amen.

STUDY NOTES

STUDY NOTES

SESSION 3

CHILDREN OF GOD

"See what kind of love the Father has given to us, that we should be called children of God; and so we are."

1 JOHN 3:1

OPENING PRAYER

Lord, come among us through your Holy Spirit. Illuminate our hearts and minds as we study your Word together. Guide us into the truth that will transform us to be more like your Son. Teach us to love you and to love one another. We pray in Jesus' name. Amen.

QUESTION
What does it mean to be a child of God?

SESSION INTRODUCTION
The deepest desire of John's heart was to see God's people walk in light, obedience, and love. Throughout these five chapters of John's first epistle, he will spiral through these three themes taking them deeper with every twist and turn.

In this section of Scripture, John called his readers to marvel at what God has done for them. The Lord has lavished his love upon them and called them his very own children. Through the work of Jesus, they have assurance of their salvation, their sanctification, and their ultimate glorification.

Just as an earthly child resembles his father, so God's children are to resemble him. A child of God will walk as Jesus did – in righteousness, purity, and obedience. John challenges his readers in this section to do a true assessment of their lives. Do their lives reflect the Lord or the devil? John would have them know that their actions speak louder than their words.

WALKING IN LIGHT
1. What do you think a life of righteousness, purity, and obedience looks like today? Has anyone modeled this life for you?

2. How does God's love motivate you towards obedience?

Watch the Video

The video teaching can be found at **biblestudymedia.com/walkinginlight**. If you are hosting this group as an online group and are experiencing diminished quality, you may need to encourage members to take time to watch the video on their own rather than try to play it through your online meeting platform.

Video Notes

True Children Speak the Truth in Love: John exemplified what it meant to speak the truth in love. John loved the Lord and loved the Lord's people. He longed for these beloved believers to have full assurance in Christ. From that place of love, John challenged his readers to examine their lives.

True Children Know God's Love for Them: Assurance grows in the Lord as believers come to really understand how the Lord loves them. With great fervor, John exclaimed that the Lord has lavished his love upon them and calls them his very own children. He longs to care for them, guide them, provide for them, and lead them in holy and righteous living.

True Children of God Do Not Sin: John would have everyone live as children of God. Nevertheless, he was not unaware of the work of Satan and all his evil forces. John went on to say that anyone who made a practice of sinning was not a child of God. John knew that a child of God would continue to sin while living in this earthly bodies; however, that child would not want to remain in sin. A true child of God would recognize his sin, confess that sin, and repent of the sin so that he could walk again in the righteousness of Jesus Christ.

True Children Practice of Self-Examination: As Christians, we must continue the practice of self-examination so that the Lord and others can see the light of Christ in our lives.

What resonated with you from the video teaching?

WALKING IN TRUTH
Read *1 John 2:28-3:10.*

3. In her teaching, Brooke differentiated between a person who sins and a person who makes a practice of sinning. Discuss the difference between these two.

4. List markers that John gave in these verses to assure a person that they have been born of God.

5. What is the significance of Jesus Christ coming to take away sins? How have you experienced his forgiveness for sin and healing from the bondage of sin?

6. The Holy Spirit has been given to the believer to enable him or her to walk in righteousness. What benefits are experienced when a believer continually responds with conviction and repentance in the Holy Spirit? What happens when we don't respond?

WALKING IN LOVE
7. John wrote that there were the children of God and the children of the devil. John would call his readers to consider what their lives reflect – God or the devil. How do these two designations challenge you? Is this kind of self-examination a part of your Christian practice? Why or why not?

8. John was very concerned about Christians being deceived (3:7). During his time, there were many heresies that arose in the church. These people either denied the deity of Christ or the humanity of Christ. What heresies plague the church today and how do you guard against these?

9. Last week, we discussed the practice of abiding and how we could incorporate more abiding into our lives. Share with the group how you incorporated that abiding last week and how you will continue to implement this spiritual practice.

PRAYER REQUESTS

You may want to share prayer requests with one another. There's a Prayer & Praise Journal found on p.184 where you can keep track of your group's requests. Have someone close in prayer or pray the following prayer together:

"Lord of all power and might, who art the author and giver of all good things: Graft in our hearts the love of thy Name, increase in us true religion, nourish us with all goodness, and bring forth in us the fruit of good works; through Jesus Christ our Lord, who lives and reigns with you and the Holy Spirit, one God, for ever and ever. Amen."

BOOK OF COMMON PRAYER, P.181

STUDY NOTES

STUDY NOTES

SESSION 4

LOVE ONE ANOTHER

"By this we know love, that he laid down his life for us, and we ought to lay down our lives for the brothers."

1 JOHN 3:16

KEY VERSE
"Almighty Father, whose blessed Son before his passion prayed for his disciples that they might be one, as you and he are one: Grant that your Church, being bound together in love and obedience to you, may be united in one body by the one Spirit, that the world may believe in him whom you have sent, your Son Jesus Christ our Lord; who lives and reigns with you, in the unity of the Holy Spirit, one God, now and for ever. Amen."

BOOK OF COMMON PRAYER, P. 255

QUESTION
What does it mean to love like Jesus?

SESSION INTRODUCTION
As John's epistle continues, he takes his readers deeper into the themes of truth, obedience, and love. John reminds his readers of the command to love God and to love one another; it was from the beginning of time and will remain to the end of time.

Jesus was and is the perfect demonstration of love. John calls his readers to follow the example of Jesus in how they love one another. In loving people, Jesus broke through all the societal norms of his day: he talked to Samaritan women, touched lepers, and shared meals with tax collectors and prostitutes.

What we learn from the life of Jesus is that to truly love others requires sacrifice. Jesus made the ultimate sacrifice on the cross. Now, we as Christians are to pick up our crosses, deny ourselves, and serve others in a sacrificial manner.

Once again, John will remind us that it is through abiding in the Lord, abiding in his love that we learn to truly love him and his people. As we abide in him, so he abides in us through his Holy Spirit. It is the work of the Holy Spirit to transform our hearts. Through that transformative power, we can walk as Jesus walked and love as Jesus loved.

WALKING IN LIGHT

1. Has anything spoken to you in this week's daily devotional readings?

2. Why is it hard to love people?

Watch the Video

The video teaching can be found at **biblestudymedia.com/walkinginlight**. If you are hosting this group as an online group and are experiencing diminished quality, you may need to encourage members to take time to watch the video on their own rather than try to play it through your online meeting platform.

Video Notes

Love Is From God: In this session, John takes us back to love. Since we have been loved by God, we are now to love one another. Love comes from God not from the world.

Love Not Hate: John tells us not to be like Cain because Cain murdered his brother. While Abel did what was right in the eyes of God, Cain did what was right in his own eyes.

Love One Another: John provided a negative example in Cain and then a positive example in Jesus. Jesus perfectly demonstrated love through his death on the cross. Because we have been loved, we are now to follow the example of Jesus and to love one another.

Love Assures: Through this demonstration of love for one another, our hearts are reassured that we dwell in God and God dwells in us.

What resonated with you from the video teaching?

WALKING IN TRUTH
Read *1 John 3:11-24*.

3. Why did John tell us *"do not be like Cain"*? What was his problem (1 John 3:12, see also Genesis 4:1-10)?

4. The death of Jesus on the cross on behalf of sinners exemplified sacrificial love. Jesus loved us so much that he gave his life for us, that we may be forgiven and in relationship with the triune God. What does this sacrifice of Jesus on your behalf mean for you personally? Do you live as one who is loved like that (3:16)?

5. How does the Lord call us to lay down our lives for our brothers and sisters? What are practical ways that we do that as a church? What are the ways you personally serve in your community?

6. How does keeping the commandment to love God and to love others lead you toward fulfilling the rest of the commandments?

WALKING IN LOVE

7. John shared three great assurances that we experience as we love others: no condemnation from our hearts (3:19), confidence before the Lord (3:21), and answered prayers (3:22). Are you living in these assurances? Which one is most meaningful to you?

8. God has gifted us all differently and given us different passions and interests. With your unique design, who are the people that the Lord calls you to see and minister to?

9. As we abide in the Lord – his truth, obedience, and love – he transforms our hearts to become more like his. How are you experiencing this transformation through this study? What will you commit to do in order to walk in the light this week?

PRAYER REQUESTS

You may want to share prayer requests with one another. There's a Prayer & Praise Journal found on p.184 where you can keep track of your group's requests. Have someone close in prayer or pray the following prayer together:

Lord, we ask that you would continue to transform our hearts through your Holy Spirit. Help us, Lord, to see people as you see them, to love them as you love them, and to live in authentic fellowship with them. In Jesus' name, Amen.

STUDY NOTES

STUDY NOTES

SESSION 5

GOD IS LOVE

"Beloved, let us love one another, for love is from God, and whoever loves has been born of God and knows God. Anyone who does not love does not know God, because God is love."

1 JOHN 4:7-8

OPENING PRAYER

"O God, you have taught us to keep all your commandments by loving you and our neighbor; Grant us the grace of your Holy Spirit, that we may be devoted to you with our whole heart, and united to one another with pure affection; through Jesus Christ our Lord, who lives and reigns with you and the Holy Spirit, one God, for ever and ever. Amen."

BOOK OF COMMON PRAYER, P. 230-231

QUESTION

What is most challenging to you about loving your Christian brothers and sisters?

SESSION INTRODUCTION

John continues in his spiral teaching of the letter starting with truth, moving to love, and concluding this chapter with obedience.

The children of God are the recipients of God's great love. Their obedience to God is then demonstrated not just in loving God but in loving each other.

John used the word "abide" four times through this short section of his letter. To abide in God means to abide in love. Abiding leads to loving.

WALKING IN LIGHT

1. What is the significance of God abiding in the believer?

2. John addressed the issue of hypocrisy in the church – when one claims to love God but hates his brother, he proves to be a liar. Do you think John was being too harsh here?

Watch the Video

The video teaching can be found at **biblestudymedia.com/walkinginlight**. If you are hosting this group as an online group and are experiencing diminished quality, you may need to encourage members to take time to watch the video on their own rather than try to play it through your online meeting platform.

Video Notes

Love Is Truth: John begins the chapter with another strong warning to his readers. They are to test the spirits in order to discern the Spirit of truth from the spirit of error. The Spirit of truth will always confess that Jesus Christ has come in the flesh. Any spirit that does not make that confession is the spirit of error and is to be overcome by the truth.

Love Discerns: John said to be discerning but then to be loving. Those who abide in the truth of God are to love one another as God has loved them. God initiated love for us then demonstrated that love through the propitiatory work of Jesus on the cross.

Love Casts Out Fear: The perfect love of God casts out fear. The children of God are being made perfect through Jesus Christ. They have nothing to fear in this life or the life to come because the blood of Jesus has made full payment for their sins. Judgment on their behalf was already done, and the punishment has already been taken on their behalf.

What resonated with you from the video teaching?

WALKING IN TRUTH
Read *1 John 4:1-21*.

3. John instructed his readers not to believe every spirit but to test the spirits (1 John 4:1-6). Why was that so important during John's time? Why is it so important today? How do you test the spirits to discern between the Spirit of truth and the spirit of error?

4. In 4:7-8, John gave the essential characteristic of a child of God—love. How can we know and understand what true love is?

5. How is the child of God made perfect? Have you experienced this perfect love that casts out fear?

6. The perfection of God's love within the believer is demonstrated by him loving his brothers and sisters. Why did John challenge the person who thinks he can love God whom he has not seen if he cannot love his brother whom he has seen?

WALKING IN LOVE

7. How are you challenged to love the difficult people in your life? How does obedience tie in to your ability to love those people?

8. What are some steps you can take this week to abide in God's love more deeply and to demonstrate God's love more tangibly?

PRAYER REQUESTS

You may want to share prayer requests with one another. There's a Prayer & Praise Journal found on p.186 where you can keep track of your group's requests. Have someone close in prayer or pray the following prayer together:

We love Lord, because you first loved us. You are the originator of love and the definition of love. Teach us to love as you have loved us. Forgive us for not loving you and for not loving our brothers and sisters as you have called us to do. Transform our hearts today through your Holy Spirit so that we may live in obedience to you. Amen.

STUDY NOTES

STUDY NOTES

SESSION 6

CHILD OF THE LIGHT

"And we know that the Son of God has come and has given us understanding, so that we may know him who is true; and we are in him who is true, in his Son Jesus Christ. He is the true God and eternal life. Little children, keep yourselves from idols."

1 JOHN 5:20-21

OPENING PRAYER

"Shed upon your Church, O Lord, the brightness of your light, that we, being illumined by the teaching of your apostle and evangelist John, may so walk in the light of your truth, that at length we may attain to the fullness of eternal life; through Jesus Christ our Lord, who lives and reigns with you and the Holy Spirit, one God, for ever and ever. Amen."

BOOK OF COMMON PRAYER, P. 238.

QUESTION
How do you keep yourselves from idols?

SESSION INTRODUCTION
As John is wrapping up his letter to the churches, he once again calls his readers to know the truth about Jesus Christ – Jesus is the one to whom the water, blood, and the Spirit all testify. Jesus is life, and Jesus is the source of eternal life.

Children of the Lord know this truth and have this eternal life; therefore, their lives are to reflect that truth and life. They are to live in obedience to the commands of the Lord and to love one another. Faith, obedience, and love all work together to assure the readers that they are truly the children of God.

Four times in the last four verses, John uses the phrase, "We know." There is certainty in Jesus; there is the certainty of eternal life; there is certainty in being the true children of God. John wanted his readers then and his readers now to embrace this certainty so that they could live in the confidence, boldness, and assurance that are rightfully theirs through Jesus Christ.

WALKING IN LIGHT
1. John said that the commandments of the Lord are not burdensome. What would you say to John about the commandments?

2. How have your views of the commandments changed throughout your journey of faith?

Watch the Video

The video teaching can be found at **biblestudymedia.com/walkinginlight**. If you are hosting this group as an online group and are experiencing diminished quality, you may need to encourage members to take time to watch the video on their own rather than try to play it through your online meeting platform.

Video Notes

Children of the Light Are Victorious: John reminds his beloved readers that they are victorious over the evil powers of this world through their faith in Jesus Christ.

Children of the Light Are Confident: John concludes his letter with the blessed assurance given to believers. They have eternal life through the Son. There is confidence for eternity but also for today. A child of God can rest in the knowledge that God cares for them, listens to them, and answers their prayers.

Children of the Light Are Devoted: The final words of John are a warning about the idols of this world. John knows that abundant life is found only in full devotion to the Lord. Anything less than Jesus Christ is a substitute for the real thing. Never settle!

What resonated with you from the video teaching?

WALKING IN TRUTH

Read 1 John 5:1-21.

3. What are the criteria that John provided for being a child of God (See 5:1-5)?

4. How is a child of God to overcome the world?

5. How do you understand the sin that does not lead to death and the sin that does lead to death?

6. Are you open to your brothers and sisters recognizing your sin and interceding for you? Discuss how love would motivate you to acknowledge sin in your community, to confront it, and to pray for it? Do you see this happening in your own community?

WALKING IN LOVE

7. Why do you think John ended his letter with the command to keep yourselves from idols (5:21, see also Psalm 115:3-8)? Why do you think we continue to struggle with idolatry?

8. How are you personally encouraged by the assurances that John shared throughout this letter? How are you growing in boldness and confidence before the Lord from this study?

9. When you think about walking as a child of the light, what does that mean to you now that you have studied 1 John? What are your hopes for this group to serve as an encouragement and support to you in your walk going forward?

PRAYER REQUESTS

You may want to share prayer requests with one another. There's a Prayer & Praise Journal found on p.186 where you can keep track of your group's requests. Have someone close in prayer or pray the following prayer together:

Lead us, Lord, in the way of truth, in the way of obedience, and in the way of love. Bind our hearts to you so that we may faithfully walk as children of the light. In Jesus' name, Amen.

STUDY NOTES

STUDY NOTES

APPENDICES
FREQUENTLY ASKED QUESTIONS

WHAT DO WE DO ON THE FIRST NIGHT OF OUR GROUP?

Have a party! A "get to know you" coffee, dinner, or dessert is a great way to launch a new study. You may want to review the Small Group Covenant (page 182) and share the names of a few friends you can invite to join you. But most importantly, have fun before your study time begins.

WHERE DO WE FIND NEW MEMBERS FOR OUR GROUP?

Finding members can be troubling, especially for new groups that have only a few people or for existing groups that have lost a few people along the way. We encourage you to pray with your group and then brainstorm a list of people from work, church, your neighborhood, your children's school, family, the gym, and so forth. Use the five circles on the next page to identify potential group members with whom you would like to build a spiritual friendship. Have each group member invite several of the people on his or her list.

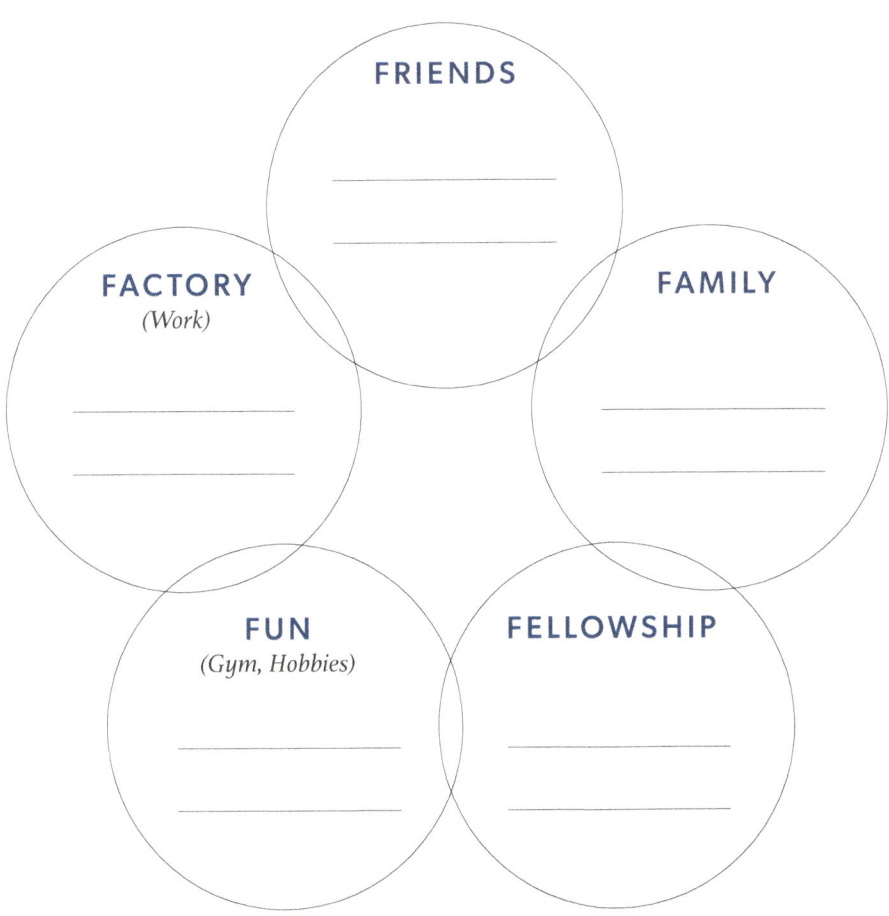

No matter how you find members, it's vital that you stay on the lookout for new people to join your group. All groups tend to go through healthy attrition—the result of moves, sending out new leaders, ministry opportunities, and so forth—and if the group gets too small, it could be at risk of ending. If you and your group stay open to ideas, you'll be amazed at the people God sends your way. The next person just might become a friend for life. You never know!

HOW LONG WILL THIS GROUP MEET?

Most groups meet weekly for at least their first six weeks, but every other week can work as well. We strongly recommend that the group meet for the first six months on a weekly basis if at all possible. This allows for continuity and, if people miss a meeting, they aren't gone for a whole month.

At the end of this study, each group member may decide if he or she wants to continue on for another study. Some groups launch relationships for years to come, and others are stepping-stones into another group experience. Either way, enjoy the journey.

CAN WE DO THIS STUDY ON OUR OWN?

Absolutely! This may sound crazy, but one of the best ways to do this study is not with a full house but with a few friends. You may choose to gather with

another couple who would enjoy some relational time (perhaps having a nice dinner) and then walking through this six week study. Jesus will be with you even if there are only two of you (Matthew 18:20).

WHAT IF THIS GROUP IS NOT WORKING FOR US?

You're not alone! This could be the result of a personality conflict, life stage difference, geographical distance, level of spiritual maturity, or any number of things. Relax. Pray for God's direction, and at the end of this six week study, decide whether to continue with this group or find another. You don't typically buy the first car you test drive or marry the first person you date, and the same goes with a group. However, don't bail out before the six weeks are up—God might have something to teach you. Also, don't run from conflict or prejudge people before you have given them a chance. God is still working in your life, too!

WHO IS THE LEADER?

Most groups have an official leader. But ideally, the group will mature, and members will rotate the leadership of meetings. We have discovered that healthy groups rotate hosts/leaders and homes on a regular basis. This model ensures that all members grow, make their unique contribution, and develop their gifts. This study guide and the Holy Spirit can keep things on track even when you rotate leaders. Christ has promised to be in your midst as you gather. Ultimately, God is your leader each step of the way.

HOW DO WE HANDLE THE CHILDCARE NEEDS IN OUR GROUP?

Very carefully. This can be a sensitive issue. We suggest that you empower the group to openly brainstorm solutions. You may try one option that works for a while and then adjust over time. Our favorite approach is for adults to meet in the living room or dining room and to share the cost of a babysitter (or two) who can watch the children in a different part of the house. This way, parents don't have to be away from their children all evening when their children are too young to be left at home. A second option is to use one home for the children and a second home (close by or a phone call away) for the adults. A third idea is to rotate the responsibility of providing a lesson or care for the children either in the same home or in another home nearby. This can be an incredible blessing for young ones. Finally, the most common solution is to decide that you need to have a night to invest in your spiritual lives individually or as a couple and to make your own arrangements for childcare. No matter what decision the group makes, the best approach is to dialogue openly about both the need and the solution.

SMALL GROUP COVENANT

OUR PURPOSE
To provide a predictable environment where participants experience authentic Christian community to grow spiritually.

GROUP ATTENDANCE
To give priority to the group meeting. We will call or email if we will be late or absent. (Completing the Group Calendar on the next page will minimize this issue.)

SAFE ENVIRONMENT
To help create a safe place where people can be heard and feel loved. (Please, no quick answers, snap judgments, or simple fixes.)

RESPECT DIFFERENCES
To be gentle and gracious with different spiritual maturity levels, personal opinions, temperaments, or "imperfections" in fellow group members. We are all works in progress.

CONFIDENTIALITY
To keep anything that is shared strictly confidential and within the group, and to avoid sharing improper information about those outside the group.

SHARED OWNERSHIP
To remember that every member is a minister and to ensure that each attender will share a small team role or responsibility over time.

ROTATING HOSTS, FACILITATORS, AND HOMES
To encourage different people to host the group in their homes and to rotate the responsibility of facilitating each meeting.

GROUP CALENDAR

Planning and calendaring can help ensure the greatest participation at every meeting. At the end of each meeting, review this calendar. Be sure to include a regular rotation of host homes and facilitator, and don't forget birthdays, socials, church events, holidays, and mission/ministry projects.

DATE	SESSION	HOST HOME	SNACKS	FACILITATOR
	1			
	2			
	3			
	4			
	5			
	6			

PRAYER & PRAISE JOURNAL

SESSION 1

_____

_____

SESSION 2

_____

_____

SESSION 3

_____

_____

SESSION 4

_____

_____

SESSION 5

_____

_____

SESSION 6

_____

_____

SMALL GROUP ROSTER

NAME	EMAIL	PHONE

SMALL GROUP LEADER HELPS

HOSTING AN OPEN HOUSE

If you're starting a new group, try planning an Open House before your first formal group meeting. Even if you have only two to four core members, it's a great way to break the ice and prayerfully consider who else might be open to joining you over the next few weeks. You can also use this kick-off meeting to hand out books, spend some time getting to know each other, discuss each person's expectations for the group, and briefly pray for each other. A simple meal or good dessert always make a kick-off meeting more fun. After people introduce themselves and share how they ended up being at the meeting (you can play a game to see who has the wildest story!), have everyone respond to a few icebreaker questions, such as:

- What is your favorite family vacation?
- What is one thing you love about your church/our community?
- What are two things about your life growing up that most people here don't know?

Next, ask everyone to tell what he or she hopes to get out of the study. You might want to review the Small Group Covenant on page 182 and talk about each person's expectations and priorities. Finally, set an open chair (maybe two) in the center of your group and explain that it represents someone who would enjoy or benefit from this group who isn't here yet.

Ask people to pray about inviting someone to join the group over the next few weeks. Hand out postcards and have everyone write an invitation or two. Don't worry about ending up with too many people; you can always have one discussion circle in the living room and another in the dining room after you watch the lesson. Each group could then report prayer requests and progress at the end of the session

You can skip this kick-off meeting if your time is limited, but you'll experience a huge benefit if you take the time to connect with one another in this way.

LEADING FOR THE FIRST TIME
SEVEN COMMON LEADERSHIP EXPERIENCES.
WELCOME TO LIFE OUT IN FRONT!

- Sweaty palms are a healthy sign. The Bible says God is gracious to the humble. Remember who is in control; the time to worry is when you're not worried. Those who are soft in heart (and sweaty-palmed) are those whom God is sure to speak through.

- Seek support. Ask your leader, co-leader, or a close friend to pray for you and prepare with you before the session. Walking through the study will help you anticipate potentially difficult questions and discussion topics.

- Bring your uniqueness to the study. Lean into who you are and how God wants you to uniquely lead the study.

- Prepare. Prepare. Prepare. Go through the session, read the section of Scripture. If you are using the video, listen to the teaching segment. Consider writing in a journal or praying through the day to prepare yourself for what God wants to do. Don't wait until the last minute to prepare.

• Ask for feedback so you can grow. Perhaps in an email or on index cards handed out at the study, have everyone write down three things you did well and one thing you could improve on. Don't get defensive. Instead, show an openness to learn and grow.

> • Share with your group what God is doing in your heart. God is searching for those whose hearts are fully his. Share your trials and victories. We promise that people will relate.

> • Prayerfully consider whom you would like to pass the baton to next week. It's only fair. God is ready for the next member of your group to go on the faith journey you just traveled. Make it fun and expect God to do the rest.

LEADERSHIP TRAINING 101

Congratulations! You have responded to the call to help shepherd Jesus' flock. There are few other tasks in the family of God that surpass the contribution you will be making. As you prepare to lead, whether it is one session or the entire series, here are a few thoughts to keep in mind. We encourage you to read these and review them with each new discussion leader before he or she leads.

1. Remember that you are not alone. God knows everything about you, and he knew that you would be asked to lead this group. Remember that it is common for all good leaders to feel that they are not ready to lead. Moses, Solomon, Jeremiah, and Timothy were all reluctant to lead. God promises, "Never will I leave you; never will I forsake you" (Hebrews 13:5). Whether you

are leading for one evening, for several weeks, or for a lifetime, you will be blessed as you serve.

2. Don't try to do it alone. Pray right now for God to help you build a healthy leadership team. If you can enlist a co-leader to help you lead the group, you will find your experience to be much richer. This is your chance to involve as many people as you can in building a healthy group. All you have to do is call and ask people to help. You'll probably be surprised at the response.

3. Just be yourself. If you won't be you, who will? God wants you to use your unique gifts and temperament. Don't try to do things exactly like another leader; do them in a way that fits you! Just admit it when you don't have an answer and apologize when you make a mistake. Your group will love you for it, and you'll sleep better at night!

4. Prepare for your meeting ahead of time. Review the session and write down your responses to each question. Pay special attention to exercises that ask group members to do something other than engage in discussion, like take an action. These exercises will help your group live what the Bible teaches, not just talk about it.

5. Pray for your group members by name. Before you begin your session, go around the room in your mind and pray for each member. Ask God to use your time together to touch the heart of every person uniquely. Expect God to lead

you to whomever he wants you to encourage or challenge in a special way. If you listen, God will surely lead!

6. When you ask a question, be patient. Someone will eventually respond. Sometimes people need a moment or two of silence to think about the question. Keep in mind, if silence doesn't bother you, it won't bother anyone else. After someone responds, affirm the response with a simple "thanks" or "good job." Then ask, "How about somebody else?" or "Would someone who hasn't shared like to add anything?" Be sensitive to new people or members who aren't ready to say, pray, or do anything. If you give them a safe setting, they will blossom over time.

7. Provide transitions between questions. When guiding the discussion, always read aloud the transitional paragraphs and the questions. Ask the group if anyone would like to read the paragraphs or Bible passages. Don't call on anyone, but ask for volunteers; then, be patient until someone begins. Be sure to thank the people who read aloud.

8. Break up into small groups each week or a larger group won't stay. If your group has a lot of people, we strongly encourage you to have the group gather sometimes in discussion circles of three or four people during the Rekindle the Promise or Renew the Promise sections of the study. With a greater opportunity to talk in small circles, people will connect more with the study, apply more quickly what they're learning, and ultimately get more out of it. A small circle also encourages a quiet person to participate and tends to minimize the effect of a more dominant or vocal member. It can also help people feel more loved in your group.

When you gather again at the end of the section, you can have one person summarize the highlights from each circle. Small circles are also helpful during prayer time. People who are not accustomed to praying aloud will feel more comfortable trying it with just two or three others.

Also, prayer requests won't take as much time, so circles will have more time to actually pray. When you gather back with the whole group, you can have one person from each circle briefly update everyone on the prayer requests. People are more willing to break into small circles to pray if they know the whole group will hear all the prayer requests.

9. Rotate facilitators weekly. At the end of each meeting, ask the group who should lead the following week. Let the group help select your weekly facilitator. You may be perfectly capable of leading each time, but you will help others grow in their faith and gifts if you give them opportunities to lead. You can use the Group Calendar (p. 183) to fill in the names of the different leaders for all the meetings if you prefer.

10. One final challenge (for new or first-time leaders): Before your first opportunity to lead, look up each of the five passages listed below. Read each one as a devotional exercise to help equip yourself with a shepherd's heart. Trust us on this one. If you do this, you will be more than ready to lead your first meeting.

Matthew 9:36
1 Peter 5:2-4
Psalm 23
Ezekiel 34:11-16
1 Thessalonians 2:7-8, 11-12

NOTES

NOTES

ACKNOWLEDGEMENTS

My first thanks and acknowledgement must go to my husband, Charlie. Charlie has been my greatest cheerleader and encourager in writing this book. He believed in me when I did not believe in myself. Charlie, your love has changed me. You have modeled the love that John wrote about throughout 1 John. Thank you for being faithful to your vows to love me in the good times and the bad times. I am so grateful for you, for our marriage, and for the ministry the Lord has allowed us to share throughout these past 26 years together.

My next thanks must go to our amazing team at Bible Study Media. I am so grateful for the love, friendship, and ministry we share together. Cathy, I love you like a sister and treasure the gift of you. Thank you for all your support and encouragement and thank you for opening your beautiful home for the filming of this study's videos. Christine, I adore you and treasure our conversations and friendship. Thank you for believing in me, giving me this opportunity to write and teach, and for all the behind-the-scenes work you did along the way. Joni, I marvel at you and give thanks for you daily! You excel at everything you do. You provide so much behind-the-scenes support and keep us on track. Thank you for being you. I am so blessed to call you my friend and colleague! Samantha, you are a true gift to our team. Thank you for bringing your wealth of knowledge and expertise to this study. I couldn't have done it without you. You are so precious to me already. Thank you also to Jereme and Chris. You two are exceptionally gifted. Thank you for your vision, for your attention to detail, and for all the work you have done to make this book beautiful.

To our board members, thank you for your ongoing investment in Bible Study Media. We are so blessed to have each one of you bringing your experience, your commitment, and your passion behind our work. Each one of you is a true gift to me and to our team.

Last but certainly not least, thank you to our many donors. We could not do this without you! Thank you for embracing the vision and ministry of Bible Study Media and thank you for investing in that vision and mission.

The Lord builds his kingdom through our collaborative work. May he be glorified through the writing and teaching and through the investment of all those who have come together to make *Walking in Light* a reality. I am truly humbled and grateful to be part of this collaborative team!

Do you ever feel yourself falling away from God?

Draw Near: Hebrews on Christian Worship is a Bible study on the Book of Hebrews intended to lead participants into a deeper intimacy with the Living God in the context of New Testament worship.

This study provides both individual daily devotion and a small group study format, and it is transformative for an entire congregation when used as a church-wide study with sermon alignment around the weekly themes.

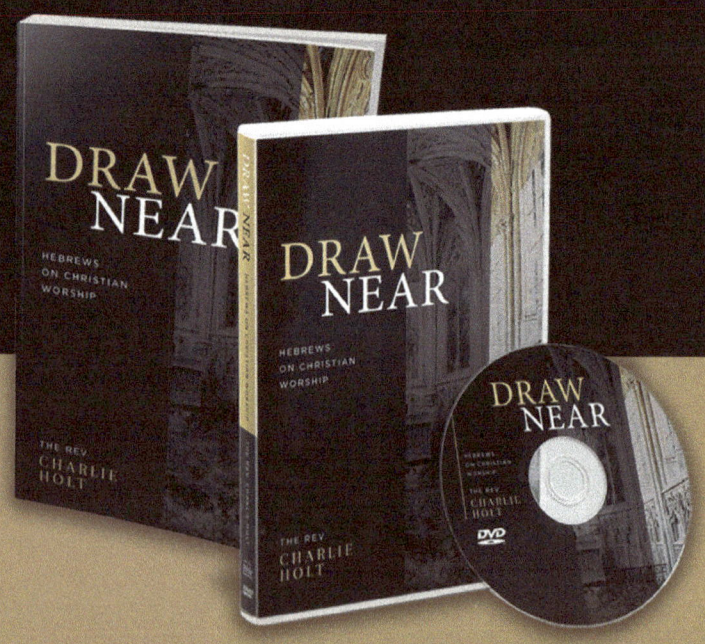

For More Information visit
biblestudymedia.com/draw-near

More cups for thirsty souls.

THE CHRISTIAN LIFE TRILOGY
The Crucified Life
The Resurrected Life
The Spirit-Filled Life

DRAW NEAR

A LIVING HOPE

WALKING IN LIGHT

TRUSTING GOD

 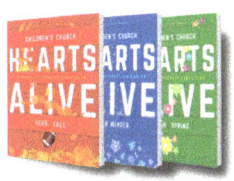 

THE CROSS WALK

HEARTS ALIVE SERIES
Children's Church
Fall
Winter
Spring
Summer

HEARTS ALIVE SERIES
Sunday School
Fall
Winter
Spring

Igniting Hearts. Engaging Minds.

biblestudymedia.com

Will you help our God create a masterpiece within the hearts of yourself and others?

We believe in building up the Church through a fresh discovery of God's Word and Spirit. We produce resources to shape hearts and minds around the patterns of Christ while strengthening the Christian community.

As we are a donation-supported ministry, any and all gifts are welcomed and greatly appreciated.

donate.biblestudymedia.com

Bible Study Media
Igniting Hearts. Engaging Minds.

www.ingramcontent.com/pod-product-compliance
Lightning Source LLC
Chambersburg PA
CBHW042112120526
44592CB00042B/2709